What Your Daughter Isn't Telling You

What Your Daughter Isn't Telling You

Expert Insight Into the World of Teen Girls

Susie Shellenberger
Kathy Gowler

GOOD TIMES BOOKS PVT. LTD.
NEW DELHI (INDIA)
www.goodtimesbooks.com

Published by
GOOD TIMES BOOKS PVT. LTD.
H-13, Bali Nagar, New Delhi-110 015 (INDIA)
Phones: +91-11-25913301, 45069086 Fax: +91-11-45069086
Email : info@goodtimesbooks.com
Website : www.goodtimesbooks.com

First Good Times Edition 2010
Second Reprint Edition 2012

ISBN-13 : 978-81-909595-0-6

Cataloging in Publication Data--DK
Courtesy: D.K. Agencies (P) Ltd. <docinfo@dkagencies.com>

Shellenberger, Susie.
What your daughter isn't telling you : expert insight into the world of teen girls / Susie Shellenberger & Kathy Gowler.
p. cm.
ISBN 9788190959506

1. Mothers and daughters--Religious aspects--Christianity. 2. Teenage girls--Religious life. 3. Daughters--Religious life. I. Gowler, Kathy, joint author. II. Title.

DDC 248.845 22

Originally published in English under the title
What your daughter isn't telling you
by Revell,A Division of Baker Publishing Group,
Grand Rapids, Michigan, 49516, U.S.A.

Printed in India at
Salasar Imaging Systems

To my precious little granddaughter

Braelyn

—you are a joy and a blessing to our family.
I look forward to pouring into your life
as you grow older, and I thank God
for the gift of your life.

—Kathy

SUSIE SHELLENBERGER is the founding editor of *Brio* magazine for teen girls, published by Focus on the Family. A former high school teacher and youth pastor, she is in demand as an international speaker and has traveled to every continent in the world.

KATHY GOWLER and her husband, Jeff, have two grown children and live in Cascade, Colorado. Kathy serves as events coordinator for teen ministires at Focus on the Family and has traveled around the world with Susie.

Introduction

We met Augie on a late summer day. Only a few weeks old, he had learned to navigate the pasture, wandering a good distance from his parents and gaining confidence daily in the big new world that lay before him.

We were doing a photo shoot for a girls' magazine, and it required a young pygmy goat. Augie was perfect. Adorable, friendly—as cuddly as a pygmy goat can be—and he instantly captured our hearts.

As his owner walked toward him calling his name, this wobbly little four-footed guy ran eagerly to follow the voice he'd come to know as friendly—the one who fed and cared for all the goats and horses in the pasture.

We were captivated.

His tiny bleating was an obvious response to the voice he knew. As he ran across the field to meet us, his mother continued grazing, oblivious to us or where her youngster was headed. The grass was tall and sweet. She too knew the voice that was calling her young one away and felt secure.

It didn't take long for Augie to notice that his master wasn't alone—there were six more of us in the pasture that day.

Although he was confident in his newfound independence around his owner, he began to get jittery among the strangers. He allowed us to pet and cuddle him, but before long he began to get nervous and squirmy.

It was obvious he was scared, and he began crying out for his safety net, his *mama*.

What happened next was precious.

Although she was enjoying the delicious grass and peaceful grazing, the instant that mother goat heard her baby bleating, her head popped up and she came *running* in our direction, straight toward her young one calling out for her.

She didn't take time to analyze the situation for danger; she just came running. Her mother-instinct told her Augie needed her *now*, and she was headed to his rescue.

What a beautiful realization that was for me. Even animals need their mamas! And what's more beautiful, our Creator gave animal mothers the instinct to care for their young—to protect them and know the difference between a playful cry and one that pleads, "Help! Mama, I need you!"

As Daisy ran toward her young one that day, we found it interesting that Augie didn't run right to her; it was enough for him to know she was there. He wasn't in danger—just got spooked and needed the reassurance that his mother, his source of protection, was nearby.

Our experience in the pasture that August afternoon reminded me once again of the importance of mothers. Our children depend on us; *need* us.

They count on us to teach, protect, and look after their well-being in a very big, frightening world.

Obviously we can't carry our daughters around with us forever or be with them every minute of every day. They need to learn to walk and talk and navigate the world on their own.

We wouldn't *want* them tethered to us for life. The natural progression of letting go begins the day we leave them with their first baby-sitter.

It's the way it must be—otherwise they'd be crippled for life, depending on us for their every need. Our children must learn to gradually move away from us to function on their own.

But they need to be prepared for that day.

That's what parents are for.

Reality

In a perfect world, mothers would have nothing more on their minds than what's going on with their children. The truth is, today's culture has many moms working outside the home, running carpools, chairing committees—juggling far more than the hours in a day can handle.

By the end of a busy day, it's all they can do to put dinner on the table, throw in a load of laundry, and make sure homework is done.

Through our CLOSER events and working with moms and teen girls around the world, we get more than a thousand emails and letters every month from teen girls desperate to talk to someone about what's on their minds.

They're asking us questions they feel uncomfortable asking their moms, but we wonder, *Why aren't they asking their moms?*

Sometimes the questions are as simple as "What's a training bra?" or "How do I use a tampon?" or "If I use a tampon, will I still be a virgin?"

We're grateful to be in a position of trust where teen girls feel they *can* ask us anything and receive an honest answer.

But wouldn't it be great if these girls could take their most intimate questions to the ones who love them more than anyone else in the world—their mothers?

Why Don't They?

Many girls don't think they can talk to their moms about certain issues. They're afraid they'll be laughed at, lectured, or belittled for their curiosity, so they go to someone else for the answers they're looking for.

What follows in this book are real questions and comments from teen girls who felt they couldn't go to their moms for whatever reason. Instead they chose to ask us—the people behind the pages of a magazine—whom they've come to know as women who will give them the truth—straight up.

There's no beating around the bush.

They write to us because they feel *safe* writing to us.

No question is too silly or embarrassing.

No one's going to laugh at them.

They know they'll get the truth—plain and simple—wrapped in love.

If you have a teen daughter, chances are good she's had many of these same questions. Maybe she asked you, maybe she asked a friend, or maybe she even wrote to us.

Whatever the case, these are questions teen girls are asking, things they're dying to talk about with someone they can trust.

These are the things your daughter isn't telling you.

Chapter 1

Why Girls Need Moms

God made men and women different on purpose. Both are essential to a healthy family. He created the male to be the protector and provider for the family. Man was created to process his decisions logically.

The female—whom God designed to bear children—is emotionally wired.

She's the "heart" of the home.

The nurturer.

The caretaker.

Mothers give life and are *life-giving* to their children.

They're the ones who wake up in the middle of the night to check on a fevered child; every whine or whimper penetrates the deepest sleep.

They're created with antennae that flash at the first sign of danger or pain in their children's lives—by God's design.

The same-sex parent is the most influential person in a child's life. Although mothers are the first to bond with their children even before birth, little boys quickly gravitate to their fathers, imitating and striving to be like them.

Little girls, on the other hand, emulate their mommies—cuddling and singing to their baby dolls because that's what mommy does.

Mommy's the one who models to her daughter what it means to be female. Her daughter learns from her how to love and nurture a family, how to respect her husband and care for her home, how to view her role in society and find her God-given purpose. Without these two very different role models to bring balance in the home, children can easily become confused about gender issues and their own sexuality. By *God's design*, they were created male and female, both essential to raising healthy, well-established children.

Because this book is written for mothers and daughters, our focus will be on the importance of the role moms have in the lives of their daughters, particularly teen daughters.

The mother-daughter relationship can be wonderfully close *and* full of tension and high emotion. You love each other fiercely, but there are also days you just may not like each other much.

Guess what—that's *normal*! You're both wired to be emotional and verbal creatures! Throw into the mix the raging hormones of adolescent girls and middle-aged moms, and you have the makings for one emotionally charged altercation after another.

Mothers often get blamed for any and every malfunction in their children's lives. Why is that? If you don't adjust socially, it's your mother's fault. She must have secluded you at a young age, and you didn't learn how to socialize with your peers.

If you're prone to getting into trouble for misbehaving in class or sassing adults, your mother must not have trained and disciplined you to behave properly.

Mothers play a critical role in the emotional and psychological development of their children. Early bonding with his or her mother, or lack of it, has a direct impact on a child's life and emotional stability. It's our relationships with our mothers—the primary caretakers in those early years of our lives—that largely determine our self-worth and how we see ourselves in relation to others as we mature.

When everyone else in the world lets us down, we all need *someone* to be there for us, cheering us on and picking us up when we fall; someone we can go to with our problems and questions who will love us no matter what. Wouldn't it be great if that person was our mom?

God Handpicked the Mother of His Son

So important is the role of motherhood that God handpicked the woman who would give birth to and raise His own Son. Scripture tells us Mary was favored not for her physical beauty or IQ, but because she was a willing servant, available to her Lord. (See Luke 1:26–38.)

She was selected by God because of her heart, her strength, and her desire to serve Him.

God knew she would have to be a special woman—someone able to endure the rumors and raised eyebrows for being a pregnant unwed teen.

He knew she needed to be strong enough to endure all that Jesus would face during His short lifetime.

He knew she would have to trust Him with her child's future, not knowing where that would lead.

She'd have to be tender enough to sing lullabies to the King of Kings—dry His tears and bandage His scraped knees—yet be strong enough to watch Him be tortured and die simply for who He was, the Messiah. Yes, God the Father knew exactly what kind of mother His Son needed to teach Him about life and prepare Him for death. He would be different from her other children, yet He needed to be treated equal to them. It would take a special woman indeed.

God also chose a special woman to raise your daughter. He gave her just the mother she would need—you.

Back to the Basics

It's important now and then to take a good look at our lives and evaluate how we're doing with raising our children. Hectic schedules may need to be adjusted, priorities realigned, and our role of caretaker and nurturer put back in its proper place on the totem pole of our lives.

We all know how important it is for young children to be with their mothers during the formative years. The truth is, that need doesn't change as they get older. In fact, teenagers need their moms in their lives perhaps more now than ever.

They're being bombarded with cultural issues and peer pressure that often we parents aren't even aware of. They live in a world far different than the one you experienced during your teen years.

They're confused about many things—from gender issues to what's expected of them by parents, teachers, and friends. They have questions they need honest answers to but may not know who to ask.

Whom can I trust?
What if my teacher's gay?
Will I be safe at school today?
Will terrorists destroy my world?

What if I'm date-raped?

Will I even reach adulthood?

What do I do about my friend who's suicidal?

Teen girls today deal with far different issues and bigger fears than their parents did growing up. Now, more than ever, our girls need someone they can go to with their questions without being laughed at, shrugged off, or ignored. Many tell us they have no one with whom they can talk about the things that concern them.

Ironically, this is the time they stop talking about their problems and close up to the adults in their lives, feeling no one cares or would understand anyway.

Young girls who used to tell their mothers everything now shut themselves up in their rooms, no longer talking about what's on their minds.

What happened to stop the communication that once flowed so freely?

Why are so many teen girls writing to virtual strangers about their most personal thoughts and feelings instead of talking to their mothers?

Here's what they're telling us about that. . . .

✉ I feel as though my whole life is falling apart. I can't make my mom happy. Everything I do only makes her mad. I try to apologize, but she doesn't take me seriously. All I want to do is cry and cry and cry.

✉ I want to get closer to my mom, but I don't have much money. Got any ideas that don't cost a lot?

✉ I'm from a big family, so I don't get much alone time with my mom. I want us to be really close, but how can we make that happen with so many others in the house? I admit, I haven't always been obedient, but I want things to change. I want us to be close.

✉ Whenever I try to talk with Mom or Dad about stuff in my life, they go wacko. I want to be able to share my problems with them, but I need them to stay calm when I tell them things. Because of the way they react to me, it's just much easier not to talk with them at all. Can you help me?

Chapter 2

"Why Won't She Talk to Me?"

Many moms feel as though their teen daughters are shutting them out, and they don't understand why. The little girl who used to tell her everything is now quiet and distant. The relationship that used to be close is now strained. What happened?

Sometimes it's just a normal stage teen girls go through—separating themselves from their mothers to find their own identities. That's completely normal. They want a measure of privacy and sometimes just need to sort things out for themselves.

Other times, though, the lines of communication have been broken and the teen daughter simply gives up and stops talking to her mom about personal things.

Some tension between a daughter and her mother as she transitions from girlhood to womanhood is inevitable. Hormones rage and emotions run high.

What's the difference between normal mom-daughter relational stress and a complete breakdown in communication? What makes a teen girl suddenly stop talking to her mom?

We'll let some of them tell you. . . .

✉ Okay, here's the deal: My mom and I never see eye-to-eye on anything. I'd love to talk with her about things—you know, questions I have, stuff I'm struggling with, relationships. I really want her to understand where I'm coming from. And I want to understand her point of view; I really do! I just long for a real mom-daughter relationship like some of my friends have. I can't imagine how cool it would be to feel close to my mom. Can you tell me how to get that?

✉ I'm the oldest in my family, and I'm twelve. My mom and I used to spend all kinds of time together—before my third sister was born. We read together, and we'd just sit on the couch and snuggle and talk. But we don't do that anymore. I felt so special when she spent alone time with me. Now I don't feel loved at all. I want us to get back to where we used to be. Is it possible?

✉ I wasn't going to tell my mom what was bothering me, because I knew how hurt she'd be. But she knew something was up. For an entire month, she kept putting pressure on me to open up with her. I admitted I was afraid she'd no longer love me when she found out what I'm dealing with. She laughed and said that wasn't possible.

So I told her.

I'm a lesbian and I have a girlfriend.

Just as I thought, she started crying. Now I wish I'd never told her the truth. She's very distant with me. We used to be so tight. I miss the mom I used to have. I want our closeness back, but I don't know what to do.

✉ Ugh! I'm so angry at my mom and dad. They've planned out my entire life — even which college I'll attend. This is my life, and they're not even asking what I think!

✉ Whenever I start to open up with my mom, I get so nervous and chicken out. I've lied, and I want to come clean with her about it. I also need to tell her about my boyfriend. But we just can't communicate. How can I change things between us?

✉ I'm TIRED. I'm tired of my sister, my mom, and life in general. Sigh. Mom doesn't listen to me when I try to talk with her. I'll start, but she changes the subject to herself. Because of that, I've just stopped talking with her. Yeah, this is selfish, but I need my mom to listen to ME and hear MY problems!

✉ I love my boyfriend; I really do. And whenever my mom gets mad at me, she threatens to break us up. So that tells me I shouldn't talk with her. Why does she use him against me to get me to do what she wants? I feel manipulated.

I also think I'm depressed. I'm borderline anorexic. I eat in front of my folks, but I never eat very much. They read my diary, so they found out I'm struggling with anorexia . . . and again, they threatened to break up my boyfriend and me if I don't start eating more.

I wish so badly I had someone to talk to! After my last fight with Mom, I started cutting myself. I feel so alone.

These precious girls have two things in common: they feel empty and lonely in their relationships with their moms, and they want better relationships but feel helpless and don't know how to fix it.

Lonely is a dangerous place for a teen girl to be, regardless of the reasons why.

If she feels she can't talk to her mom about what she's feeling without being laughed at or ignored, she'll find someone else to talk to—or more frightening, another way to deal with her pain.

For some it becomes an eating disorder—when the rest of her life seems out of her control, she controls the only thing she can: what she does or doesn't put into her body.

Others turn to Internet relationships and find strangers who show interest in them and don't judge them. There's always someone online available to listen, comfort, and make a lonely girl feel loved.

Too many lonely teen girls will give themselves to the first boy who looks their way, simply because they long to feel cared for and accepted.

We're not saying that every girl who gets involved in these kinds of behaviors does it because of her mom. There are many godly women who are heartbroken and pray daily for their daughters who may be involved in a harmful relationship or behavior; there can be a multitude of reasons for a young girl to make unhealthy choices.

Take note! If you're turning a deaf or critical ear when your daughter is trying to talk to you, she may easily feel rejected and look elsewhere for the comfort she's seeking. Teen girls are in an emotional, turbulent time of life. All too often it's easy for adults to simply shrug off what to a teen is a heartbreaking, life-or-death situation. They desperately need someone to listen to their sometimes not-so-obvious cries for attention.

✉ I love my mom to pieces, but it's really tough to talk about girl things with her. I've tried asking her advice about makeup and dating, but she just looks at me like it's not important. It hurts when she laughs at my questions. I'd give anything in the world to have someone in my life who could give me good advice and who would just love me in spite of the fact that I have so many questions.

✉ I'm the only girl in my family, and I'm also the oldest child. It seems my mom and I can't get along anymore. Somehow we always end up in a fight. I've tried to get advice from my dad, but he won't even listen to me.

So I started writing notes to my mom. I've even apologized to her. But when I tell her I love her, she just says, "Yeah," and then walks away. I don't know what else to do!

What Kind of Mom Are You?

In the busyness of life, you may think you're in tune with your daughter, but are you really? It may surprise you to discover that from her perspective you don't have a clue about what's going on in her life.

How can you tell if you're doing a good enough job of being there for her? Start by asking yourself these questions:

When your daughter talks to you, do you really listen, or are you distracted?

God gave moms the amazing ability to do ten things at once. You can be cooking dinner, feeding the dog, ironing a blouse, and making a mental grocery list all at the same time your daughter is telling you about her most horrible day at school.

Make a point to stop what you're doing and look her in the eye when she's talking to you. Let her *see* that you are really listening to her. Give her your full attention. If you appear distracted she'll feel she might as well be talking to a tree. Tune in to her when she talks to you—let her know that what matters to her is important to you.

Can your daughter trust you?

✉ Know why I don't talk to my mom anymore? She goes right to her church friends and tells them everything I've told her!

Mom, your daughter needs a safe place to share her heart. You're blessed if she feels comfortable doing that with you. If that trust is broken, it can sometimes be irreparable. It's sacred and worth protecting.

You see, it takes more than just *saying* she can tell you anything. You also need to *prove* to your daughter that you *are* a safe place to share her innermost feelings. If you've ever blown it in this area, you know it can take months to rebuild that trust.

Vulnerable young girls will quickly clam up if they find their private talks haven't been kept private. Be careful not to betray her confidence when she tells you something personal.

Remember when you were her age? It's not easy for young girls to talk about intimate things with their parents, and they can be easily embarrassed. Take extreme caution to protect her confidentiality. It will either encourage your daughter to be more open with you, or it will slam the door of communication shut.

How are you doing?

Take a moment to reflect on the level of communication you have with your daughter. Maybe it's not all her fault if there's stress between you. Be honest.

- *I encourage my daughter to bring her questions to me, and she knows I'll give her honest answers.*
  ______*True*______*False*

- *My daughter knows she can trust me and is comfortable sharing personal things with me.*
  _____*True*_____*False*

- *This is a weak area for me. I sometimes share with others things she's told me in confidence.*
  _____*True*_____*False*

- *We don't keep secrets in our family. She should know that anything she tells me I'll tell her dad.*
  _____*True*_____*False*

Probably the best way to find out how you're doing in the area of trustworthiness is to ask your daughter! And when you do, encourage her honesty. She'll let you know if you're a safe place for her.

Tell Her You're There for Her

To develop or maintain open communication with your daughter:

- Assure her that *no* question is too embarrassing, off-limits, or dirty. She needs *someone* whom she can ask her questions to and receive honest answers. Let her know you're there for her and want to be that person.
- Don't assume she knows you invite her questions if you haven't told her so. Make it clear that she can come to you with anything at any time.
- Make sure she knows that no matter who else lets her down or doesn't seem to care, you are always there for her—that she can always come to you for help, guidance, or just a lap to lay her head on and cry if she needs to.

You are your daughter's only mother—she needs you to be that person in her life.

Which describes you?

A. *My daughter knows I'm her biggest cheerleader and am always there for her.*

B. *I want to be an approachable mother and need to make some changes to be sure my daughter knows I'm available for her.*

C. *I'm already too busy and don't have time to baby her. She's a teenager and should be more responsible for herself and solving her own problems.*

It's easy to assume our daughters know things we haven't really told them. Make sure your daughter knows beyond all doubt that you're there for her. If you aren't comfortable saying it verbally, write her a letter and leave it on her pillow, or send her an email telling her how you feel.

Again, the more you let her know that you care about what she's going through, the easier it will be for her to open up and talk to you. It may be awkward at first, but it will get easier, and the payoff will be worth all the effort!

Chapter 3

Actions Speak Louder Than Words—What Her Silence May Really Mean

Maybe your daughter has stopped talking to you yet her behavior screams *something's wrong!* It's possible she's desperately trying to say something but just doesn't know how, so she acts out instead.

It's easy to overreact to this behavior or ignore it completely, missing the reasons for it. Be careful not to overlook obvious red flags.

It's important to pay attention to behavioral changes and really listen to what your daughter may be communicating without actually saying it. There are many reasons teen girls shut down, especially if they feel no one cares or sees their pain. Sometimes the pressure is just more than they can handle, and parents need to take that seriously.

"I'm Depressed"

✉ I feel broken, and I'm only thirteen. I'm never happy, and I cry all the time — even during the night. I'm on the swim team, and I love swimming. But this year there was a price increase to participate, and we just don't have the money. I hate missing out on being with my friends on the team. I really miss it a lot! Swimming helped me keep in shape. Now I feel fat and like I don't fit in anymore.

✉ My life is really messed up. Dad lost his job, so Mom had to find work. We're probably going to have to leave the house we're in, and my brothers are jerks to me. Mom and I are constantly fighting. I just want to die right now! My family has no money, and I only have a couple of friends. If this is how life is going to be, I don't want to keep living.

✉ I've thought about suicide for the past year. I pray, but I can't hear God. I usually can't feel Him, either. I'm trying to follow Him, but it sure is tough when I'm depressed. Is He really here?

✉ Sheesh! My life is completely out of control! No one understands me — especially not my family. They yell at me every day, and because of that, I cry a lot. I've been having stomach problems and headaches, and I'm starting to wonder if God really does have a plan for my life.

✉ I hate life, and I hate my life. Whatever I do, it's never good enough for my parents. All they do is yell at me. They come home tired from work, and they're always in a bad mood. I'm thinking about running away from home. If my parents don't enjoy being parents, why'd they even have children?

Girls today are living in a crazy, pressure-filled world, and because of that, depression has become nearly epidemic. If your daughter says she's depressed, take her seriously and help her get to the bottom of it.

Here's what the National Youth Violence Prevention Resource Center has to say about teenage depression: "Depression can lead to poor school attendance and performance, running away, and feelings of worthlessness and hopelessness. Some teens try to make the pain of depression go away by drinking or taking drugs, which only makes depression worse. Still others contemplate suicide."*

There's a difference between being "depressed" because she didn't get asked to the dance and being physically and clinically *depressed*.

How do you know the difference? Look for these symptoms:

Symptoms of clinical depression

- Sad or irritable mood
- Loss of interest in activities that were once enjoyable
- Changes in appetite or weight
- Difficulty sleeping or consistent oversleeping
- Loss of energy
- Feelings of worthlessness or guilt
- Difficulty concentrating
- Frequent thoughts of death or suicide

Other signs to watch for

- Frequent headaches, muscle aches, stomachaches, or tiredness, without a medical cause

***www.safeyouth.org/scripts/teens/depression.asp*

- Frequent absences from school or poor performance in school
- Talk about or efforts to run away from home
- Boredom, sulking
- Lack of interest in spending time with friends or family
- Alcohol or substance abuse
- Social isolation or poor communication
- Fear of death
- Extreme sensitivity to rejection or failure
- Increased irritability, anger, hostility, or crying
- Reckless behavior
- Neglect of clothing or appearance
- Difficulty with relationships
- Changes in mood[†]

According to the NYVPRC, "it is entirely normal to feel 'blue' occasionally, or to feel down for a while after something bad happens. . . . Most teens experience some of these symptoms occasionally."[‡]

But if your daughter has a number of these symptoms for more than a few weeks, she may be clinically depressed and need professional help. It's important to know that depression isn't a sign of weakness—it's a medical illness and can be treated.

These signs can also be indicative of other problems such as an eating disorder or a chemical imbalance. Check with your family physician if you suspect your daughter may have depression. It's possible that her depression can be treated

[†]Ibid.
[‡]Ibid.

with medication. Be open to professional Christian counseling if needed as well.

How common is depression among teenagers?

The NYVPRC states that "major depression strikes about one in twelve adolescents. In any given six-month period, about 5 percent of nine- to seventeen-year-olds are estimated to be suffering from major depression."[§]

"I'm Lonely"

✉ I feel as though I'm a prisoner inside my own home. I've been homeschooled all my life, and I don't really have any friends. Our church is tiny and full of old people, and we live in a really small town. What hope is there for me?

✉ I'm wondering if there's anyone in existence who's more strict than my parents. They won't let us attend movies or hang out at other places where teens are. The closest church with a youth group is twenty miles away from us. Mom and Dad say that's too far to drive. So what can I do? I feel as though I'm dying!

✉ I belong to a homeschool group, but I'm the only teen. I'd love to have some friends my age. Our church doesn't have a youth group, so I go to Sunday school with my parents. I've tried to talk them into letting me find a church with a youth group so I can have some friends, but they say we have to attend the same church, and this is the church they've chosen. Ugh!

[§]Ibid.

These girls desperately want to be connected with other teens. Learning how to interact socially with their peers is vital to healthy emotional development.

When we read emails like this, we assume the parents are trying to do what's best for their teens, but they're overprotective out of fear. They're afraid that outside influences will harm their children if they're not in complete control of their lives.

The truth is each time our daughter walks out the front door, she *will* be influenced by forces we can't control. Parents have a huge responsibility to protect and prepare their kids to face those influences, and it can be very intimidating.

Keeping your daughter so sheltered from the outside world that she's denied experiences essential to learning how to interact socially and deal with peer pressure may do her more harm than good.

Again, we receive countless emails and letters from teen girls around the world. And, as you can see, many are dealing with overprotective parents. Yet if we were to ask these parents if they were sheltering their teens, they'd more than likely respond with a no. So the problem is not simply being overprotective; it's often not realizing or being willing to admit that they're hindering their teens by doing so.

Please don't misinterpret this. Our teens definitely need protection. And we hope you're actively sheltering them from immoral or unhealthy influences. But allow us to repeat: There *are* times when—out of fear—parents build an overprotective shell around their children.

How do you know if your protection is excessive? Respond to the following questions by answering true or false. (We'll use "she" or "her" in place of "my teen daughter" throughout this quiz.)

____ 1. She doesn't relate well to her peers.
____ 2. I haven't allowed her to spend the night in another home.
____ 3. She's uncomfortable around other teens.
____ 4. She has no interests outside the home.
____ 5. I haven't allowed her to participate in a week-long camp or missions trip.
____ 6. She's awkward socially.
____ 7. She isn't able to articulate the reasoning behind our rules.

If you answered "true" to the majority of these questions, would you consider the possibility that you're an overprotective parent who could give your daughter a bit more freedom?

And as you *gradually* expand her boundaries, pray for discernment to know when to pull back and when to release.

> ✉ We had to move to a different state, and I totally miss the friends I'd known my whole life. I'm miserable here. I don't fit in at school, and yes, I've tried to make new friends. No one pays any attention to me. Or if they do, they look at me like I'm a freak.
>
> Mom says things will eventually get better. I don't have eventually. I need friends now! Why can't she understand how incredibly lonely I am? I'm desperate. I wish I could die!

Moving is traumatic for teens. Suddenly they're uprooted from all that's familiar. School and friends are their lifeline to social survival. Suddenly having to start over with all new people can be terrifying and difficult.

Our family (Kathy here) learned this the hard way. My husband's career in the corporate side of the home-building business can mean frequent moves; we go where the market is hot at the time. Several years ago that meant moving our family to the other side of the country when our kids were eleven and fourteen.

We'd moved before, and it wasn't a big deal then. This time, however, for our middle-school–aged son, it was a very traumatic experience. He'd been a leader in his former school, had lots of friends, and was active in all kinds of church and school activities.

In our new city, though, things were very different. The culture was difficult to penetrate for newcomers.

When Matthew wore his Colorado Rockies shirt to school, he was slammed against his locker. He was in different territory, and these students definitely weren't Colorado Rockies fans.

As an eighth-grader, he had an assigned seat in the school cafeteria because of the disciplinary problems with the students. He had to sit every day at lunch with kids he would never have chosen as friends and had nothing in common with. In fact, they were the type of kids we'd taught him to stay away from.

He was miserable—even came home in tears some days. He was desperately lonely, and it caused great pain for the whole family.

My phone calls to the school voicing my concerns fell on deaf ears. After a few months when nothing was getting better, we had to ask ourselves some tough questions:

- What are we doing here?
- Is any job worth this kind of pain and heartache for our teenage son?
- We are hundreds of miles away from grandparents, friends, and a church in which we were very involved. What do we really want for our kids at this time in their lives?

Long story short, after much prayer and soul-searching, my husband quit a job he enjoyed with a promising future, we backed out of a deal on a new home that was being built, and we packed up and moved home—back to Colorado. No jobs, no home, but knowing in our hearts we had done the right thing for our family.

For us, it was the right decision. We started over.

It wasn't easy, but God blessed our faithfulness to do what was best for our kids and their well-being.

As a result, Jeff started his own business, and God has blessed it. I went to work for Focus on the Family and have had amazing ministry opportunities that have taken me around the world the past eleven years.

Matthew has met and married the love of his life, and they now have a precious baby. Thankfully, our daughter, Kelly—who's extremely social—was hardly fazed by the whole thing. For us, moving back was the best thing we ever did.

Although family moves are sometimes necessary because of job transfers or other circumstances, it's a decision that needs to take into consideration the whole family—particularly your teens. Their lives depend on friendships, fitting in, and *belonging*. For them it's a matter of survival. Some can transition without so much as a hiccup, but for others, it can be devastating, with far-reaching repercussions.

There are other reasons teens feel lonely, but the worst kind of loneliness is being in the midst of a crowd of people yet not feeling connected to anyone. Can you relate? Technically you're there physically, but emotionally you feel alone, like nobody notices you or even cares that you're there. The following email says it well. . . .

✉ Okay, here's the deal. I don't want to go to some cheesy counselor. I admit, I need to talk with someone, but I'm afraid if I tell anyone what I'm dealing with, they'll make fun of me or make me get counseling. Aren't there supposed to be all kinds of trusted adults for teens to talk with? How come there are NONE in my life? I soooo wish I could tell someone how I feel without being judged.

"I Don't Feel Loved"

⌧ My mom says she's too weak to take out the trash, but she disciplines me with her hand. How can she be strong enough to hit me but not able to lift a trash bag? Yeah, she's been sick a lot the past couple of years, and because of that she's changed. We fight a lot now. She yells so loud, it's frightening. I don't even know if she loves me anymore. I feel like I'm just being used to do chores and to help take care of her. Is this abuse?

⌧ My family's a mess! I'm wondering why my parents even had children. They sure don't seem to enjoy us! They just boss us around and complain about how much money we cost them. They send us to our rooms a lot, and they fight nearly all the time. I'd love to run away, but I don't know where I'd go. I also feel as though I need to be here for my little sister and brother.

⌧ I know you're going to say I'm too young for this—I'm thirteen—but I want to have a baby really really bad! I just want someone to love and love me back, and a baby will do that for me.

Whether it's due to neglect, sibling rivalry, or just a lack of communication, feeling unloved by your own family articulates loneliness beyond description. If your own parents don't show you love, what choice do you have but to search for it elsewhere?

For too many teen girls it means running into the arms of the first guy who pays attention to her and "promises" to love her. Sadly, too many times a girl like this finds herself pregnant and alone when her source of love dumps her for someone else.

To love and be loved is a basic human need. Some girls—like the thirteen-year-old who wants a baby—will do anything to feel loved. Obviously she's thinking of her own need to be needed and not considering the consequences of what having a child at such a young age means.

In her young, inexperienced mind, a baby will fill the void in her life—until she realizes when it's too late that a baby isn't a puppy. You can't give it away when you're tired of it. She's not thinking about how a baby requires constant care, feeding, and responsibility, let alone the financial cost of raising a child as a single teen mom.

How do these girls get to such a point of desperation? They told us themselves: they feel unimportant and unloved by their parents.

Chances are, if we were to ask these parents if they love their daughters, they'd say, "Of course! She should know that!" But somehow between juggling the stresses and struggles of life, the message was sent out to these girls that their parents don't love them or are too busy to pay attention to them.

We can't assume that once we get our kids through the infant and preschool stages, they can exist on autopilot or their emotional needs are met. Even if your family is on the tightest of budgets, you can lavish them with the security of knowing they're precious to you and loved beyond words. That's a gift we can all afford, and it's something our children desperately need from us.

"I'm Afraid"

✉ There's a guy in one of my classes at school who keeps looking at my breasts. He says weird stuff all the time, like, "You look like a country girl, and I like country girls. I'm gonna teach you how to ride a horse." I get scared whenever I have to go to this class. How do I get him to leave me alone?

✉ No one understands how terrified I am to go to a new school next year. I'm afraid I won't fit in. On top of that, I'm a cutter. I'll try to make friends, but I'm not sure how. People say, "Be yourself." I don't even know what that means. I wish my mom would help me.

✉ My fears dictate my thoughts and actions. I'm really an insecure person, and I've always thought men were mean. But since being in high school, I've made some guy friends who have helped change my mind. But I'm still scared of allowing a guy to truly care about me. I'm so scared, I'm starting to avoid guys who are nice to me. I want God to use me, but I feel He can't as long as I'm so paralyzed with fear. I mean, how could I ever get married? I feel as though I'm the worst person in the whole world.

✉ I'm so scared something is going to happen to my mom at work or when she's going to the grocery store, etc.

Remember a couple years ago when the Amish children got shot? It was all over the news. Well; I knew the man who shot those children. Now I feel like I can't trust anyone.

I feel sorry for my family, because I never want us to go out and have fun. I just want us all at home together. I'm not even interested in doing anything with friends. I just want to be home and have my family right there with me. Worry has taken over my life.

✉ Yeah, it was stupid, but my friend and I took inappropriate photos of ourselves and showed them off in chat rooms. Now a guy at my school is threatening to blackmail us with the photos. I'm afraid of what he might do with the pictures. I'm afraid to talk with my mom about it. What should I do?

These are some heavy fears for young girls to deal with alone. Letters like this make us wonder if parents have any idea what their daughters are dealing with at school.

Many teen girls don't know what to do with sexual harassment, emotional or physical abuse, or bullying. They need to know that they should report these types of behaviors to school administrators, counselors, or if needed, the police. Doing the right thing could save another girl from experiencing the same terror.

These types of incidences shouldn't be taken lightly. Unfortunately, reporting them can have negative consequences for the victim. It's important for you, the parent, to realize that reporting peers to authorities is an extremely traumatic thing for your daughter to do. She'll need your support and possibly even protection for a while to make sure she's not further victimized by the person she reported.

If you haven't already done so, sit down and talk openly with your daughter about sexual misconduct and what she can do to protect herself. Make sure she knows her rights when it comes to reporting such incidences, whether the perpetrator is a peer, teacher, or other trusted adult. She needs to know that sexual harassment is a crime, and victims are protected by law.

How much do you know about what your daughter goes through each day at school?

Is she bullied?
Has she been a victim of sexual harassment?
Does she go to chat rooms on the Internet?

The best way to find out is to ask her. Initiate conversation in a nonthreatening way—while you're in the car driving her to practice, or when you're together in the kitchen cleaning up after dinner. You may be surprised by what she tells you, but talking about it will give her security in knowing that you are there for her should she ever be victimized in some way.

> ✉ Please tell me what to do! I don't have anyone to talk with. My mom just finished training for the National Guard. She was away for six months! I missed her so much. I'm glad she's back, but all she does is complain about what she's been through and she says she doesn't feel like she fits in with our family anymore.
>
> I try to talk with her, but she gets mad. I know I'll never be able to understand all she's been through, but I need her! Doesn't she realize my dad, brother, sister, and I have all been through a lot too?

> ✉ My mom's addicted to drugs. It's been half a year since we've seen each other. I'm so worried about her, it's making me physically sick. I'm frightened she's not coming back to us . . . or she's going to die. I've tried calling her but can't reach her. I'm so scared!

> ✉ I don't think God is answering our prayers. See, my mom got very sick; she's not getting any better. We're all scared. I can see the fear in her eyes. Don't tell me everything's gonna be okay. I'm old enough to know things may not turn out okay. I need someone I can talk to. I'm so scared! What if she dies?

Fear can be a crippling emotion—especially for a young girl without much life experience. When unexpected things come our way, we all need a support system to help us navigate difficult times. When your mom is your support system and she seems to be falling apart, what's a girl to do?

It's a fact: People become physically and mentally ill. Parents die. *Mothers* die, leaving behind children and husbands to try to face life without them. I (Kathy) personally identify with this more closely than I ever imagined I would as a teenager.

My mom was diagnosed with cancer when I was sixteen. My faith in God and His power to heal was strong. I had no doubt that God would heal her and she'd be well again. Sadly, my family didn't talk about the seriousness of her illness. I had never known anyone with cancer before, and terms like *malignant* and *chemotherapy* were foreign to me.

I'll never forget that November day when my life was forever changed. I walked out of my high school to find my pastor and brother-in-law waiting for me by my car. They'd come to tell me that my mother had just died.

While I was sitting in class, my mother died!

I was numb with shock. It couldn't be! How could I not see it coming? Why had no one told me how ill she really was?

I just *knew* God was going to heal her and my life would return to normal.

But God had not chosen to heal my mom on this earth. Instead, He took her to heaven three weeks after my eighteenth birthday. I was devastated.

Sickness is real. Fears for loved ones who get sick are real. Teenagers need and deserve to hear the truth about the seriousness of a family member's illness—especially their mother's.

Well-intentioned adults may try to protect teens from undue fear and the stress of a very serious illness, but the reality is God doesn't heal every mother on this earth who gets sick.

How I wish someone had been honest with me when my mother was dying. Being a naïve and self-centered teenager, I wasn't aware of the seriousness of her condition. I regret that

I never got the chance to say good-bye. She was just suddenly gone, and life as I'd known it was over.

Teenagers are smart and deserve honesty. They can handle much more than they get credit for. Many face difficult family situations and have to grow up much too soon. More than ever, these teens need the love and support of their family and friends. The loss of a parent can be overwhelming at such a young age. No matter how well they may appear to be doing on the outside, you can be sure they are hurting deeply on the inside.

Pay careful attention to the teen in your life who's faced traumatic pain, abuse, or loss. She can become very good at hiding the inner pain that will eventually come out, one way or another.

Chapter 4

What She Wants You to Know— "I Have Questions I Don't Know How to Ask You"

"About My Changing Body . . . Am I Normal?"

✉ I don't understand when I'm going to develop. I'm way behind. Someone said there are stages in development. What are they? I feel like my hormones are going crazy.

✉ I'm so sick of looking like a boy! All my friends have breasts and are getting curves. Am I always going to look like this?

✉ Help! My breasts are two different sizes, and they're really sore. Do you think I have cancer?

✉ I sure sweat a lot! Is something wrong with me?

✉ I'm scared! There's this white stuff in my underwear, and it's really itchy down there. My friend says I need to go to the doctor. I need to tell my mom! But how can I? How do I just bring something like this up in conversation?

✉ My friend says I shouldn't wear a bra to bed. Will it stop me from growing? Sometimes I just want to sleep in my bra. Is that really bad for me?

✉ Some people say that wearing thong underwear is a sin, and others say it's no big deal. Hey, it's just underwear. Is it wrong for me to wear it?

✉ How do I find the right bra size? And what's a training bra?

✉ I want to start shaving my legs, but I'm afraid my mom will laugh at me if I ask her about it. Or even worse—she might tell me I can't shave yet. What should I do?

Puberty can be a frightening time for your daughter. Talk to her about the changes she'll experience as her body develops.

Don't wait for her to ask questions. Chances are she's feeling self-conscious and uncomfortable talking about the way her body is changing. By initiating the conversation, you'll make it easier for her to talk about things she may have been too embarrassed to ask on her own.

Let Her Know What to Expect

Things such as:

- Her breasts will start to develop and may not grow evenly at first. She may experience soreness and itching—this is *normal*. Take her bra shopping and explain how to find a good fit. If you don't know what a good fit is, ask a trained department store clerk to teach you both.

- She'll probably experience a growth spurt before her first period and feel very clumsy and awkward until she grows into herself.
- Her hips will become a bit more curved and her waist more defined.
- She'll develop pubic and armpit hair about the same time her breasts start to develop. Her legs will get hairier as well. Decide together when the appropriate time is for her to shave. If she's self-conscious about hairy legs, *run*, don't walk, to the store and buy her a razor, and show her how to use it without cutting herself. Some battles just aren't worth fighting. Something as simple as letting her shave her legs can save her huge embarrassment and the two of you unnecessary battles.
- As hormones and oil glands switch into high gear, her face may break out. Teach her to use cleansing products that will help avoid serious acne. Talk about the importance of keeping her face and hair clean. Make it a fun shopping trip as the two of you compare products that will help keep her young skin and hair beautiful. Doing this together will reinforce your closeness as you *celebrate* her growing up.
- Menstruation usually begins between the ages of ten and fourteen. Help her understand that these are *average* ages. If she's a late bloomer, she shouldn't be alarmed if it's slow in coming. She may experience a vaginal discharge before her first period and may need to wear a panty liner. Prepare her with pads and liners *before* she has her first period. Don't make her ask!

Adolescent girls are extremely self-conscious about their changing bodies. They're uncomfortable about how they're developing . . . or *not*.

Be understanding and supportive when your daughter complains about her clothes not fitting, her face breaking out, or just feeling awkward. Give her affirmation and support as she morphs from a gangly little girl into a lovely young woman.

Puberty affects the whole family. Be prepared for emotional outbursts, tears, and doors slammed in anger. Your daughter isn't turning into a monster—at least not permanently. She's struggling to find her independence. She wants space from you and is seeking room to grow. She desperately needs you, although she may not tell you.

"My Period"

✉ What if I'm at school or in some other public place when I get my first period? I'm terrified! I don't have a clue what to expect. Will everyone know that I got it?

✉ My sister hasn't gotten her period yet, and she's in high school. So does this mean it's going to take this long for me too? My breasts have started growing, and I've had a discharge. Does this mean it's about to happen? My best friend already has her period, so I want mine too!

✉ I have totally irregular periods. What's wrong with me?

✉ I HATE having a period. I just started, and I've been cramping a lot. This is ridiculous. What can I do to feel better?

✉ I don't know how to use a tampon. Are they dangerous? What if it gets lost up there?

☒ I'm afraid my mom will get all weird on me when I ask her to get me some pads. No, I haven't started my period yet, but I want to be ready. I wish she'd talk with me about puberty. I don't know what to expect. Isn't this her responsibility?

☒ Big problem: I attend a private school, and we're not allowed to carry purses. I just got my period. How am I supposed to carry protection with me? We have a pad machine in the bathroom, but it's usually empty. I don't have pockets in my uniform, so I have no clue how I'm supposed to carry stuff with me.

☒ Is it going to hurt to have a period?

☒ I want to ask my mom about tampons — will I still be a virgin if I use them? How do I insert one? I don't know how to bring this stuff up with her.

☒ Will I cramp even worse if I shower or take a bath during my period?

☒ I'm scared to death I'm going to start my period and not know what to do! I'm in the sixth grade, and I'm twelve years old. I'm afraid to talk with my mom about this, but I have so many questions. She probably knows the answers, but I'm scared to talk to her about it.

To an adult woman who experienced puberty years ago, these may seem like silly questions, but they're real questions girls have asked us. *They truly don't know about these things and want someone they can ask without fear of embarrassment*.

Really, how *are* they supposed to know if nobody talks about it with them? Some schools have a basic sex ed or health class, but most adolescent girls don't feel comfortable asking their teacher personal questions. That's why it's *so* important, Mom, for you to step up to the plate and *make* it easy for your daughter not only to discuss these things with you but also to feel confident in asking you questions.

Here are some helpful tips to prepare your daughter for her first period

- Agree ahead of time how she can tell you when her period starts. Make it as easy for her as possible to communicate with you without making it a big deal. Even asking you for more pads when she runs out can be awkward if you haven't talked about it beforehand. And remember, do NOT announce to the family that she has now "become a woman"! Remember when you were her age? Nothing could be more horrifying.
- She may have a vaginal discharge a few months before she has her first period and will have to wear a panty liner. Supply her ahead of time so she's prepared.
- Assure her that it may take several months for her periods to become regular. Demonstrate how to keep a monthly calendar so she's not caught by surprise.
- Explain the difference in feminine products and how to use them. Invite her to come to you when she's ready to try tampons.

So what are these girls really saying?

"I'm scared."

"I don't have anybody I can ask who won't laugh at me or make me feel uncomfortable."

"I've heard things from my friends I wonder about."

"What can I expect?"

They can't say it much clearer. Your daughter needs you to talk to her about womanhood and what to expect. To keep it from being awkward, start early with simple conversations while she's still a little girl. Talk about where babies come from and what puberty is. It will be more natural for you to discuss the deeper issues that are sure to follow.

Don't wait for your embarrassed young daughter to approach you and initiate these conversations. Remember, you're the life-teacher who has introduced her to so many things—her first bicycle, the first day of school, how to make friends and be a friend. Now as she enters puberty, she needs to learn from you what becoming a young woman is all about.

Know How to Start

You may feel stuck here, especially if your own mother didn't make it easy for you to ask her questions about your changing body. Try these suggestions to help get you started:

- Find a few other moms with daughters the same age as yours and invite them to form a "Girls Only" group. Plan an activity once a month to do something fun together and create a comfortable tone to have conversations about puberty, sex, dating, etc. Start slow and keep it casual. As the girls (and you) get more comfortable talking about girl stuff, it will become easier for them to ask questions and discuss personal things. Make it fun. Go out to dinner or complete a craft together so it's not so awkward to start a conversation. For practical helps and discussion starters, try starting a mother-daughter book study together. We recommend *Bloom: A Girl's Guide to Growing Up* by Focus on the Family and *Mother and Daughter—Closer to God and Closer to Each Other* by Susie Shellenberger. Trust us, the girls will love it!

- Make it easy to share. Talk about what it was like when you were her age and how you learned about puberty. It doesn't have to be a big deal—start a simple conversation with your daughter while driving in the car (just the two of you) or doing household chores together. Begin with something like, "I never felt comfortable talking with my mom about things like menstruation or my changing body. I hope you know you can feel free to talk to me about anything you don't understand."
- Be the icebreaker. Take every opportunity to make casual comments around your daughter about female things. Let her know if you're cramping or having PMS symptoms. She needs to realize this is normal and simply a part of being a woman. Be careful, though, not to make menstruation sound dreadful—you don't want to scare her to death!
- Start talking early about your family genetics. If you're a family of late bloomers, let her know so she doesn't wonder why her friends have started their periods and she hasn't. Tell her at what age you started developing. Chances are her body will follow much the same timeline as yours did at her age.
- Don't wait for your daughter to start forming breast buds before talking about how her body will be changing during puberty. She wants to know what to expect. They may be sore and itchy and develop unevenly at first. All these things are normal, and she shouldn't be embarrassed.
- If her school is having a sex ed or health class that deals with issues of puberty, ask her how it was and if her questions were answered. Did they address issues such as abortion, teen pregnancy, and STIs (sexually

transmitted infections)? When you initiate these conversations, she'll know that these topics aren't off limits and you're open to discussing them with her.

It's up to you, Mom, to set the tone for these types of conversations with your daughter. Help her understand that you know she'll have questions and she can come to you at any time for truthful answers. Be her safe place for any question she may have about her sexuality, her body, or words she's heard that may be new to her.

Chapter 5

Sex and Dating

✉ Does a woman get pregnant every time she has sex?

✉ I danced with a guy at a school party, and he kept pressuring me to kiss him. Nothing happened, because I didn't give in. But it scared me and excited me at the same time. I want to talk about it, but my mom would go crazy if I told her. I'd probably never get to go to another party the rest of my life.

✉ My friends say that it's okay to have sex before you're married. I've been taught that this is wrong, but I'm beginning to wonder if all sex outside of marriage is wrong? I've decided to wait until I'm married to have intercourse. But what about the other stuff—feeling each other, oral sex, and just sleeping next to each other? Deep inside I think it's all wrong, but I'm not sure why. No one has specifically explained to me why it's wrong.

✉ My boyfriend and I rub against each other, but we've never gone all the way. Could I get pregnant by doing this?

✉ I think sex is gross. I'm just twelve, and maybe I'll change my mind when I'm older, but maybe not. I'm just curious: Do I have to have sex when I'm married? What if I don't like it? I want to have children, but I can't imagine having sex.

✉ My boyfriend and I are sexually active, and he doesn't want me to get pregnant. What kind of birth control should I use?

✉ I'm going to be attending a state university, and the possibility of being date-raped is what scares me the most. What kind of signs should I look for in a guy who's prone to date-rape? How can I guard against this?

✉ I'm fourteen and my friends are all dating. I'm not allowed to date until I turn seventeen. That's three more years! I'm scared to death that a guy is going to ask me out between now and then. What will I say? Should I try to get my parents to change their strict rules?

✉ My boyfriend isn't a Christian but I am. I love him, but I know I can't spend the rest of my life with him. I feel trapped. How can I break up with him and not hurt him?

✉ I got to be pretty good friends with a guy in my youth group. My parents misinterpreted our friendship as dating, but it wasn't a dating relationship! They won't let me hang out with him anymore. It's breaking my heart, and now he completely ignores me.

✉ My youth pastor announced that we're going to have a series on dating and sex. I don't want the guys in the same room with the girls when we talk about this. I'm not comfortable with it at all. In fact, I'd rather not even go, but I don't want to miss church and being with my friends. What should I do?

✉ I've never had a boyfriend! My best friend is beyond beautiful and gets asked to everything. Is something wrong with me?

How do I know that God has someone for me? I really want a guy to notice me and treat me special.

✉ I have really high standards and a solid relationship with Christ. I'd never go out with a guy who's not a Christian, and I'd never allow myself to be in a compromising situation. I'm really mature for my age, and I've never given my parents any reason not to trust me.

But Mom and Dad have said I can't date until I've graduated from high school. Got any advice on how I can convince them my priorities are in the right order and I'm not going to be disobedient to God or to them?

✉ Most all the girls at my school ask guys out. My mom says that's backward. She thinks a guy should always be the one who does the asking. My girlfriends call guys all the time. Mom won't even let me do that. What's wrong with making a phone call and just talking with a guy? Is that being forward? If I wait for the guy to make the first move, he may never make it! Then what?

✉ Some people say it's wise to date a bunch of different guys in order to gain a lot of experience. What do you think?

✉ Mom says when I am ready to date, I have to do the courtship thing instead. We are fighting about everything. Shouldn't dating or courtship be my choice? It is my life!

✉ My mom and I have talked about sex a lot. I get that it's great during marriage, and being sexually involved outside those boundaries brings all kinds of problems. Mom keeps talking about how important it is that I stay pure. But I am pure! Why does she keep talking about it?

✉ Some of my friends have decided not to even kiss until their wedding day. Is a kiss before then wrong? Don't get me wrong; I'm saving sex until marriage. I just don't want to have to wait until my wedding day to kiss a guy. Is that bad?

✉ I'm scared to death! My boyfriend and I just had sex, and afterward we realized his condom had broken. What if I'm pregnant? I know what I did was a sin, and I've already asked God to forgive me. I want to talk with my mom, but I'm afraid she'll yell at me and tell me how disappointed she is. What's your advice?

✉ My boyfriend and I are engaged. We're both seventeen. We're not getting married for three more years, but we're sexually involved with each other. At first I rationalized it: I'm going to marry him, I thought. So what's the big deal?

But lately, it's been eating away at my heart. I used to wear a beautiful purity ring that my parents gave me for my sixteenth birthday. Now I'm wearing my fiancé's engagement ring, and I feel as though I've completely cheated myself out of everything I'm supposed to experience on my wedding night. I feel sick inside. It wasn't supposed to be this way.

Sex and dating are the two most common subjects we get questions about from teen girls. We live in an extremely sexually explicit culture where teens are encouraged to experience a variety of sexual activities. Most teens don't consider anything other than intercourse as being sexually involved.

Sixteen-year-old Maggie had been going out with Joe for just two weeks when he began pressuring her for oral sex. "It's not real sex," he said. "You can't get pregnant."

Many of Maggie's friends had bragged about oral sex, and she was curious. *If I can't get pregnant*, she thought, *what's the big deal?*

The next time she and Joe went out, she agreed to do what he wanted. Guess what—it was only a matter of time before she gave away her virginity. She figured as long as she had done *this*, she might as well go ahead and do *that*.

Yet if Maggie had been asked if she was sexually involved when she was still in the stages of only oral sex, she would have denied it, because "we weren't having intercourse, so I didn't consider it sex."

Oral sex has exploded among teens and even preteens. (No thanks to school assembly speakers who promote "anything goes as long as you practice safe sex. And here are some alternatives to intercourse.")

Molly innocently wore a colored thin rubber bracelet to school one day. "It was no big deal. I bought it on our family vacation last summer," she said. But Erik and a few other guys *made* it a big deal when they noticed her in the cafeteria at lunch. Word quickly got around that Molly offered specific sexual favors. She later learned from a friend that certain colors of gel bracelets were an unspoken advertisement of what a girl would do with a guy.

It was then that Molly began to notice the number of bracelets—and their specific colors—that many of the girls in her school were wearing. "I had no idea my bracelet represented something so twisted," she said. "I stopped wearing it after I found out what the guys were saying about me."

Stacia knew the party at Zack's house would be different, but she didn't *understand* the difference until she arrived. Guys and girls quickly paired up and became intimate. But they didn't stay that way for long; they switched partners and everyone was available to one another.

"It's called FWB," Megan said. "Friends with benefits."

"I've never heard of that," Stacia admitted.

"No problem, girl. You'll catch on."

Friends with benefits allows guys and girls who aren't dating each other to enjoy the sexual benefits. In other words, it's the frills of a sexual relationship with no actual relationship. No strings attached. Sexual exploration of one another's bodies without commitment.

Is it any wonder our daughters are confused? They're bombarded with an array of sexual enticements through all forms of media, as well as from their own peers. They naturally have questions about what they're seeing and hearing.

In this "anything goes" day and age, teens struggle with knowing what's moral and immoral.

They question their parents' values and rules about how old they should be before they date, courtship vs. dating, and the list goes on and on.

As your daughter tries to discover her individuality—where she fits and who she'll become—she may become very resistant to anyone, including you, telling her what to do and how to do it. This can create a minefield of emotional tension. Mom, you'll be tempted to interpret this resistant behavior from your daughter as rebellious. Have you considered that she may just be trying to figure things out for herself? Head butting, raised voices, and slammed doors may be the only communication you have with her during this turbulent time.

Too Young to Date?

Teens are beginning to date at a much younger age now than even five years ago. Girls as young as eleven or twelve write to us about how lonely they are and how they want a boyfriend like many of their friends. They perceive they are the "only ones" without a boyfriend, and from their perspective it looks so warm and fuzzy and romantic.

I (Susie) co-hosted a national call-in radio show for teens that was produced by Focus on the Family. *Life on the Edge Live!* ran for more than seven years, and it was an exciting ministry to teens through the airwaves. I can't tell you how many times I received calls from girls twelve and thirteen who were already dating and were calling with questions about relationships.

One night, after what seemed like the bazillionth call from a girl much too young to be dating, I tried something different in my approach. Instead of simply suggesting she wait until she was older to date, I put my foot down. "Okay, Samantha, back up. You're telling me you're dating Troy. You've said the two of you have been going out for a month, but I need you to clarify: What do you mean by 'going out'? You sit together in the school cafeteria? You're with each other at a school football game? What do you really mean when you say you're going out?"

"We're dating," she said. "We go out on dates."

"Just the two of you?" I pressed.

"Sure!"

"And you're how old?"

"Twelve."

"Do you realize you're much too young to be dating?" I asked.

"Oh, I don't think so."

"You're twelve!"

"So?"

"Do your parents know you have a boyfriend?" I asked.

"Yeah, and they're totally cool with it."

"Okay," I halfway chuckled. "This is really hard for me to believe. I want to talk with your parents. Put them on the phone."

"They're not here," she said.

Maybe they really weren't. But I longed for the opportunity to chat with parents about what could possibly be a good reason to allow a twelve-year-old girl to be in an exclusive relationship and to be alone on dates.

What *is* the appropriate age for dating? That's really up to a girl's parents. They know her emotional maturity level better than anyone. But when girls begin dating before the age of sixteen, they often become bored with simply dating by the time they're eighteen, and they want more. Please be wise in granting your daughter permission to date. There's simply no harm in waiting!

Communication

The thing that scares us as much as anything is what we hear from college-age girls who don't have a lot of dates or have never had a boyfriend. Too often they'll say yes to the first guy who shows interest in them out of fear of spending life alone. They don't have the experience to know that being married to the wrong guy is worse than not being married at all.

Mom, please tell your daughter every day of her life that she's beautiful, valuable, and special. Every young woman craves hearing this from *somebody*. If she doesn't hear this all-important affirmation from you, she'll fall for the first guy who pays any attention to her at all.

It will be easier for both of you if you clarify early on what your expectations are on important topics such as what is the appropriate age for dating, dating vs. courtship, curfews, etc.

Be prepared and invite discussion. Your daughter wants more than "because I said so," or "that's the way it's going to be in this house." She wants to know *why* you've established the rules you have. Take the time to explain your reasoning and share what you've learned from your own life experience.

This can be an enlightening conversation if you take the time to think through how your responses may be interpreted. Try to remember how *you* felt when you were her age and your parents' rules seemed way too strict.

Be open to compromise when appropriate. Your daughter needs to know that you're sensitive to her feelings and the pressures she feels to be accepted, while at the same time you're protecting her from harmful situations.

She may have heard you say a million times that you're simply looking out for her safety. Don't be afraid to share stories of people whose lives have been affected by bad choices or lack of parental influence. Sometimes sharing family secrets can be a good way for our kids to learn from the mistakes of others. Talk candidly about the consequences that come as a result of decisions made in a moment of teenage passion. Nobody is exempt from temptation—not even your precious little girl.

Family Connections

Yes, many young teen girls *are* lonely, but it's not because they don't have a boyfriend. Many of them just need to feel *connected* to and *loved* by someone. Mom, your work schedule may keep you from being as available to your daughter as she needs you to be. Are there things you can cut out of your life during these critical teenage years that will allow you to be there for her when she needs you most? Think about it. Is chairing that committee more important than being there for your young daughter?

Young girls especially are vulnerable to loneliness—they can't drive and are often stuck at home waiting for a ride to anywhere to get them out of the house.

Family time is especially crucial during these middle-school years of your daughter's life. Keep her busy doing fun things with you so she doesn't have time to feel isolated and lonely without a boyfriend. Recruit her help in planning a family night once a week. Use this time for just that: a designated evening specifically designed only for your family. Need help getting started? Here are some ideas:

- *Pj's and Pizza*

Select one night a week that's reserved to just stay at home and be together enjoying pizza and a good movie that everyone will like.

Put on your favorite jammies, grab a blanket, and settle in for an evening of family flicks!

- *Hot Fudge and Fun*

Head to your favorite ice-cream spot for some frivolous family feasting. Make this an intentional stop on your way home from the mall, or pile the whole gang into the car "just because." Nothing fancy, no agenda. Mentally shift into low gear and enjoy a spur-of-the-moment treat! Celebrate just being together!

- *Extended Family Ties*

Get together with extended family consistently for old-fashioned fun! Take advantage of snowy days—pull out the sleds and call the cousins, head to the park to play Frisbee, or go to each other's houses for board games. How about making nachos afterward? Don't forget older aunts, uncles, and grandparents! They have stories to share that will teach your daughter volumes about life. Promote family loyalty and build relationships with those family members nearby.

- *Become "Fan"-atics!*

Be her biggest fan. Make it a big deal to attend the sporting events or music recitals in which your daughter is involved. You'll build a strong family bond as you cheer her on and show support for her talent. Make it a family priority—be there for each other and show your support. Brothers and sisters, aunts, uncles, grandparents, cousins—make your daughter's activities a big deal for the whole family. She'll soar with confidence knowing you're in the stands. Reward her hard work with your presence.

- *Celebration Sundays!*

Before the family heads back to school and work on Monday, make a point to gear up for the next week. Designate Sunday night to regroup as a family. Enjoy your favorite finger foods, make popcorn, watch home movies, do your nails, pack school lunches, go to bed early. Take advantage of this time to savor the last of your weekend together. Touch base on the next week's activities. When is that test? If your daughter has a part-time job, what's next week's schedule? What nights will you all be home for dinner? Pray together as you head into a new week.

Your middle-school–aged daughter may often feel stuck at home with the family when she'd rather be socializing with friends, so be creative in making family time fun and active.

Open your home

Adolescents are social creatures—they want and need to be with their friends more than they want to be at home with Mom and Dad. Your daughter can't *wait* for the freedom that driver's license will bring when she won't be solely dependent on you to drive her places.

Provide fun alternatives for her when some girls her age may already be into boys and dating. Open your home to her friends. Host weekend slumber parties. Teens love spur-of-the-moment activities. Don't worry that your house may not be clean.

Keep ingredients on hand for quick and easy teen-friendly meals and snacks. A pot of chili and a pan of warm brownies is all it takes to have girls' night in! If you're a planner, put a theme together: host a "spa night" complete with manicures, pedicures, facial masks, chick flicks—the works! If you *really* want to get into it, have a candle-making or bath-salts-making party. Do girly things—everybody loves to be pampered! This would be a great time to initiate conversation with your daughter and her friends about modesty, peer pressure, and boys. Teen girls love to talk; all you'll need to do is listen.

Make your home a fun place for teens. Keep your door open to them. You'll have plenty of quiet evenings in a spotless house after they're grown and gone.

When She Starts Dating

Watching your precious—and somewhat naïve—daughter walk out the door for her first single date may be traumatic for you. You're no longer the chaperone making sure speed limits are followed, curfews are paid attention to, and most of all, her heart is protected.

You wonder if her date will treat her with respect. Will he pressure her to do things she doesn't want to do? Will he have any clue how hard you've worked to protect her all these years?

Have open discussions with your daughter about a variety of things a testosterone-driven boy might say to fulfill his sexual appetite. Together, create appropriate responses for the following.

- "I can make you feel really special if you'll let me."
- "My parents are gone and I'll be home alone tonight. Come over and keep me company."
- "No one will ever know."
- "Don't you love me?"
- "I love you; let me show you how much."

Your daughter deserves to be treated with respect and needs to know how to respond to sexual advances. It's your responsibility to prepare her and protect her from unhealthy male attention.

How do you do that? Talk to her *before* she starts dating about what healthy and unhealthy relationships look like.

Here are some red flags the two of you should watch for in an unhealthy dating relationship:

Dating Danger Signs

- He's possessive and extremely jealous.
- He accuses her of flirting when she's not.
- He tries to control how she dresses, what she does, and with whom she associates.
- He has mood swings, getting angry and yelling one minute and being sweet and apologizing the next.
- He disrespects her parents' rules and curfews.
- He tries to keep her away from family and friends.
- He threatens to hurt her.
- He threatens to hurt himself or commit suicide if she breaks up with him.
- He pressures her to be involved sexually.
- He yells, grabs, pushes, or throws things when he's angry.
- He drinks or uses drugs.
- He tells her he loves her early on in the relationship.
- He has a tragic home life. His parents abuse alcohol or drugs.

Remember: You're the parent; your daughter's the child. You're the one with the life experience. She counts on you to protect her, though she may never verbalize it. Mom, don't be afraid to *be* the parent. She'll thank you for it someday.

Restoration

✉ I heard a teen guy give his testimony about being a virgin and not wanting to date a girl who is damaged goods. He made it sound like once something's damaged, it can't ever be made good again. I was sexually active before I became a Christian. Does this mean I'm damaged goods and can't ever been seen as pure again?

✉ How does God view a girl who's been raped? Is He angry at her? Does He no longer see her as a virgin?

✉ What should I do if I get raped? I know I'm supposed to go to the authorities, but how do I handle it spiritually?

✉ I'm really shy around guys. I think it might have something to do with being sexually abused by one of my parents' Christian friends when I was younger. I know I should talk to my mom about it, but how do I bring it up? I don't want this to affect my relationship with guys the rest of my life.

✉ I've been strung out on drugs, and I've been drinking for a couple of years now. I'm sixteen and feel like my life is totally out of control. Oh yeah, I also gave away my virginity to a guy I thought loved me.

God has been working on my heart, and I'm beginning to realize how far I've wandered from Him. I've asked God to forgive me, and I believe He has. I'm going to church again and trying to live in obedience to Him. I know that someday I want to marry a Christian guy and have children. But what guy would ever want me now?

A girl who's lost her virginity because of sexual abuse needs desperately to hear this: *You were a victim of a crime*. God isn't *mad, nor does He blame you for what happened. He sees you as pure—and it was outside of His will that this happened to you.*

Girls who willingly gave up their virginity can also find a "second virginity" through asking God for forgiveness and by turning away from premarital sexual activity. There's no such thing as "damaged goods" in God's eyes.

If you know a girl who's feeling like she's gone too far and God can't—or won't—forgive her, she needs to know that God's arm of love and restoration is not too short to reach her. In fact, Christ *died* to wipe away her sin. Forgiveness can be hers for the asking.

Please don't ever let a hurting girl feel like she's a lost cause or too dirty to be cleansed. Redemption is a beautiful thing!

Chapter 6

Pornography

✉ I used to think lust and porn was a guy's problem. But I'm female, and I have a major problem in this area. I went to an online porn site and got hooked. Sex is practically all I think about. It's as though I'm consumed with it. I'm willing to talk with someone because I know I need help, but I don't know who to go to.

✉ Help! I masturbate. A lot. And I've been doing it for several years. Why do I feel so guilty about something I can't control? Why did God make me this way? Is it even possible to stop?

✉ I was sexually abused when I was five years old. Now I'm sixteen, and I battle with lustful fantasies. I'm pretty sure this is coming from what my abuser did to me. I feel a need to control all the males in my life. This is probably also connected to the abuse, right? I've never told my mom or dad about the abuse. After all, it was eleven years ago. How come I'm not over it by now?

✉ I'll be blunt. I have a strong sex drive, and I masturbate. I've tried to stop, but I can't. I feel like a hypocrite calling myself a Christian and struggling with this. I don't know who to talk to. I feel so guilty!

✉ My parents would flip if they knew this, but I'm a missionary kid and I'm addicted to cybersex and pornography. I need help, but I can't talk to Mom and Dad because it would truly break their hearts. I feel like I'm caught in a steel trap and can't get out. What can I do?

✉ I've never had sex, but I've had orgasms by masturbating. I wish I'd never done this, because it feels good and I don't know how to stop. I like how it makes me feel physically, but I hate how it makes me feel emotionally—guilty and ashamed. I even dream about sex at night. I can't stop. Help me!

✉ I've prayed and prayed and prayed about one specific area in my life. I can't stop it. I keep masturbating. Why won't God take away my desire for this? I've really tried hard to stop, but I just can't quit. I feel as though this is taking over my life. It's become a monster that's eating me alive.

✉ I'm going out on a limb here. I've decided to tell my mom about my problem with masturbation. I'm telling her because I really, really, really want to stop. I soooo hope she won't tell the rest of our family about this. Is it okay if I ask her to keep it a secret between the two of us? My parents always say we're a family with no secrets, but I don't even want my dad to know.

✉ Last year my parents took me out of the Christian school I was attending and put me in homeschool. I guess you'd call it homeschool. My mom and dad both work, so it's not like anyone's home to actually teach me. It's just me behind a computer all day. It's been tough, because I'm totally a people person, and now I'm alone for eight hours every day. So here's the deal:

Problem #1: I'm lonely.

Problem #2: I met an older girl online and started emailing with her.

At first we just talked about normal everyday stuff; then the conversation gradually shifted. She told me she's in love with me. I was bored being home alone all day, so I went along with it. Now I'm in way over my head.

She's telling me she's a sex slave to an older girl, and she's involved in pornographic photography. She's offering me $500 a week to join this little ring.

I hate admitting this, but I'm kind of enticed by it. Finally, I'd have friends again, and I'd have lots of money too.

Are you shocked at what you've been reading? These are our church kids—girls involved in youth groups, girls participating on mission trips. Don't be fooled into thinking they live in a Christian bubble and are protected from frightening influences outside and even *inside* your home.

Addiction to pornography is no longer a man's problem. Young girls often get swept into it innocently by surfing the Internet; sometimes they even come across it by accident while doing research for homework. The guilt and shame that follow are nearly unbearable, as you've read from these emails. We have a lot to cover in this section. Let's talk briefly about masturbation and move on to pornography and cybersex.

Masturbation

It's not just a guy's problem; from emails we receive on the subject, teen girls struggle with masturbation too, and they often feel alone and guilty about practicing what they consider to be a "secret sin." Some don't even know how to articulate what's happening—only that the physical sensation can become a pleasant addiction that at the same time makes them feel bad.

Christian ministers have a variety of opinions on this highly controversial subject. Some condemn it as sin, while others believe that because it isn't mentioned in the Bible, it may not be as big a deal as others think it is.

As your daughter moves into the hormonal adolescent years and you begin talking with her about the physical changes her body will be experiencing, it would be a good time to mention budding sexual desires as well.

Make it easier to approach this somewhat uncomfortable topic by explaining that God created all humans as sexual beings, and that His plan is for sexual fulfillment to be experienced in the intimacy of marriage.

It's natural for teenagers to think about sex and wonder what it will be like. They're exposed to innuendo and blatant references to sex in nearly every prime-time television show or movie they see. Of course they wonder what it's like—our culture portrays sex as a recreational activity that everybody's experiencing often. Even the most dedicated Christian teens fight battles of temptation when it comes to wanting to experience sexual pleasure.

Dr. James Dobson, esteemed Christian psychologist, addresses the subject that many consider taboo by saying there's no scientific evidence that this act is harmful to the body. As for emotional consequences of masturbation, he believes only four circumstances should give cause for concern. Those are oppressive guilt (becoming convinced that even God couldn't love them for such a "despicable act"), obsession with the act, addiction to pornographic material, or when it's carried into adulthood and becomes a substitute for healthy sexual relations between a husband and wife.

As you talk openly with your daughter about human sexuality as a gift from God, she'll be less likely to become confused about what is sin and what isn't. Encourage her questions. Answer them honestly. If this is difficult for you, here are a couple of good books you can read and discuss together:

Preparing for Adolescence by Dr. James Dobson (available in Christian bookstores)
Bloom: A Girl's Guide to Growing Up edited by Susie Shellenberger

Cybersex and Pornography

Perhaps you've heard the term *cybersex* but don't understand what it is. Cybersex is when a person becomes involved in sexual conversation and activity with another online via computer. It's defined as "the consensual sexual discussion online for the purpose of achieving arousal or an orgasm."*

Chat rooms abound for the lonely teen guy *or* girl who needs someone who will listen and make them feel important. It seems safe—no risk of STIs (sexually transmitted infections), unwanted pregnancy, or AIDS. Ideal for a lonely girl with her own computer, right? After all, she's not giving up her virginity, and no one has to know.

Until recently, men dominated the Internet world of cybersex. Now women (and teen girls) are online as much as men. Why? Women seek relationships—men pornography.

It's easy for a teen girl to justify cybersex. After all, she reasons, it's not *real* sex. The sad news is that many girls quickly become sexual addicts. Most consider themselves still sexually pure because they haven't actually had intercourse.

---

*pscharts.com/cybersex.htm.

Meet Brooke. Her parents are missionaries, and she eagerly talked to us about her relationship with Christ. And because she felt we loved her and accepted her, she confessed her sexual addiction.

"I can't help it," she said through broken sobs. "I got into cybersex through my computer, and I'm addicted. I feel desired when I'm doing it. But afterward, I always feel dirty."

Brooke was genuinely repentant and confessed that she desperately wanted to break free of her cycle of sin. We prayed with her, held her, and mapped out a plan for her to follow. Part of the plan for teens to gain victory over addiction is always to reveal the secret to parents. She had a lot to deal with!

Fortunately, Brooke's parents reacted as Jesus would. They enveloped her in love and forgiveness, then set up concrete boundaries for very limited computer use in an open area of their home. They developed a process for accountability.

Brooke was a Christian. She was sincere about her relationship with God and wanted to share her faith with others. But even as a Christian—and as a missionary kid—she wasn't exempt from sexual addiction.

Guess what! Your daughter isn't exempt either. Mom, will you be proactive? Instead of hearing about your daughter's sexual addiction after she's confessed it to others, would you set boundaries in place right now?

Yes, your control over her online use is limited; you can't oversee her computer activity at school, in the library, or at a friend's house. But by establishing solid guidelines—and explaining the reason behind them—you can take preventative measures against negative Internet activity. By talking openly with your daughter about this area of temptation, you'll also teach her that it's okay to talk with you about this.

How Can You Protect Your Daughter?

- *Be smart*. Don't allow your daughter to have a computer in her bedroom. Keep the family computer out in the open where you can monitor what she's accessing. Place the computer so you're easily able to view the screen instead of the back of the monitor.
- *Invest in protective software*. Many companies have created family-friendly software that allows you to block access to adult sites and other inappropriate areas. McAfee and Norton both offer a product called ChatChecker by Tri Synergy. It secretly captures and records both sides of instant messages and chat room conversations. Also, check into *Netsmartz.org* and *I-safe.org*.
- *Set limits*. Regulate the amount of time your kids spend on the computer each day and limit their computer usage to homework needs if necessary. Establish ground rules early on as to how much time is spent in front of the screen.
- *Warn your daughter about the dangers of Internet "surfing."* A teen girl will often innocently stumble onto pornographic sites while looking for something else on the computer and instantly become hooked. Ask your daughter if she's ever accidentally landed on provocative areas of the Internet. Mom, be the initiator. *You* start the conversation; it's unlikely that she will.
- *Don't leave your daughter alone to do homework on the computer*. Be nearby, where you can monitor her computer activity.
- *Review the Internet history and the temporary Internet files on her computer* to find out where she's going on the Web.

It only takes one accidental landing on a porn site to pull a curious teen girl into the web of Internet porn and cybersex. Again, be proactive in protecting your daughter from a lifetime of sexual addiction and bondage. Determine *right now* to protect her from that painful trap.

Chapter 7

Family Issues

✉ I think my mom loves my sister more than me. I feel like a baby even admitting this, but I want to be loved more by her. When my sister and Mom are together, they have so much fun laughing and talking. But when it's just my mom and me, it's dead silence. We can drive in the car for a solid twenty minutes and never say a word. I feel as though Mom doesn't want to talk with me or even be with me.

✉ It's so obvious that my mom favors my brother! Even other people have mentioned it to me. I can't understand why my mom does this. It makes my sisters and me feel like we don't measure up. My brother never has to do anything around the house, and he gets away with everything. Shouldn't our chores be balanced equally? And shouldn't we all be loved the same?

✉ Everyone compares me to my older sister, and I'm really tired of it! Everything she touches turns to gold. She can play the piano and the guitar, and she's good at track. She also has lots of friends and makes good grades. I'm shy and not good at much of anything. How can I get people to notice that I'm special too?

✉ I can't help comparing myself to my gorgeous sister who's popular, smart, has a great personality, and is super fashionable. I try really hard not to be jealous, but it's like I'm living with a live Barbie doll! She gets all the attention. No one even notices me when we're together. Why didn't God give me some of the good stuff?

Mom, here's a perfect opportunity for you to actively help build your daughter's fractured self-esteem. It's hard for her not to compare herself with others who seem to have it all, *especially* when it's a sibling.

If this situation rings true in your family, be sensitive to your hurting and deflated daughter. It's not fun living in anyone's shadow. Take an honest look at the relationship you have with all your children.

Do you show favoritism to one over the others? It may be more obvious than you realize, or it may be imagined. Your daughter will notice whether or not you're fair and consistent in how you treat the whole family.

Take special care to help your daughter find her gifts. God makes each of us unique—we all have talents; some may just not be as blatantly obvious as others.

Your daughter needs affirmation for the things she does well. Maybe it's writing, sewing, or painting. She may have a tender heart toward children or the elderly.

I (Susie) remember meeting Mother Teresa on a trip to India. Outwardly, she wasn't considered a beautiful person; certainly no Barbie doll. Yet I think she's the most beautiful person I've ever met. I couldn't help notice her simple sari (traditional dress/wrap worn by Indian women—and she owned only three of these), her old, worn-out sandals, and her gnarled fingers.

Mother Teresa had developed a lifestyle of truly helping, giving, and serving the poorest of the poor. She lived for the destitute and the dying. She personified the love of Jesus for those around her. Those gifts—helping, serving, and loving—usually won't put someone on a magazine cover or make someone a star. Yet she was known around the world. At the snap of a finger, I imagine she could have commanded an audience with any king, president, or dictator. Guess what—your daughter may have some of those same gifts!

Mom, if your daughter comes up lacking when she compares herself with her sister, remind her lovingly that true beauty comes from the heart. Talk about Mother Teresa. Read and discuss her biography.

Consider also reading Proverbs 31 together and discussing the Bible's description of a treasured woman. "Pretty" washes off with soap and water; "beautiful" comes from within.

✉ My family really needs your prayers. We're not speaking to each other, and we're Christians!

✉ My mom and dad are divorced. Mom is about to remarry, and she wants to have another baby! Her new marriage is a big enough transition without adding another family member to the mix. I'm hurt and confused and don't know what to do.

✉ My mom is rude to people and it embarrasses me. I no longer respect her. I know it's God's will for us to honor our parents, but how is this possible when she's so mean to people? I don't even want to be seen with her!

✉ I'd give anything to be able to talk to my mom, but every time I share something personal with her, it backfires. If I admit I'm crushing on a guy, she'll dive into a lecture on how bad that is. I'm tired of her speeches, so I've learned to stop telling her things.

✉ My mom and I have nothing in common. We disagree on almost everything, and we're always fighting. Because I'm adopted, my friends don't understand where I'm coming from either. There's no one I can really talk to!

✉ I love trendy clothes and torn jeans, but Mom doesn't. As a result, she won't let me wear any of the things I really like. We don't agree on anything, and we can't even talk without getting into a fight.

✉ My sister and I can both do the same thing, but guess who gets in trouble? I get grounded, and my sister doesn't. My mom always seems mad at me. I'd love to hear her tell me what I do right, how talented I am, or that she loves me.

✉ How can I respectfully tell my parents to mind their own business? They want to know everything! It's like our discussions are just a bunch of questions from them. Even when I talk on the phone, they have to know what I'm talking about and who I'm talking with. Can't anything be private? I'm not doing anything wrong.

✉ My parents believe that adults are always right, so they won't admit making mistakes or even discuss things with me. It's whatever they say goes! I hate it. Things are so unfair. No one can always be right! Why can't they just admit they're not perfect? I'd be a lot more open to talking with them if they'd just be real.

✉ My mom never encourages me. She started yelling at me today, so I locked myself in the bathroom. I'm under a lot of pressure. I've tried to tell my family that I don't feel loved by them, but they won't listen to me. What can I do?

✉ My mom and her new boyfriend fight all the time. I'm scared he might hurt her. I don't know what to do!

✉ I've always heard that marriage is sacred — that it's of God — and that husbands and wives should treat each other respectfully. My parents fight, and they fight hard. They've been to counseling, but it didn't help. I'm beginning to think I never want to get married.

✉ When is it appropriate to stop obeying my parents? I'm eighteen and graduating from high school in two months. I won't disobey them simply for the sake of disobeying. I'm talking about things we really disagree about. I feel I should be able to make some of my own decisions now.

✉ My sister got pregnant before she graduated from high school. Even though I'm totally unlike her, my parents are afraid that this will happen to me too. How come I have to suffer because of her mistakes?

✉ My brother has disrupted my entire family. He calls me bad names, and he's into all kinds of trouble. He does drugs, he smokes, and he threatens my mom and me. I'm starting to HATE him. We never have enough money for stuff I need because we spend it all on him. I don't think that's right! I work hard to get good grades, I make good choices, and I never cause any problems. Why am I suffering for the trouble he's causing?

Families come in all shapes and sizes with all kinds of unique dynamics. It's not unusual for an emotional and hormonal teen girl to view her parents as irrational and unfair.

We hear about two extremes: (1) "My parents don't care and are too busy to be involved in my life," and (2) "My parents are overprotective, unreasonable, and have unrealistic expectations."

It could very well be that some of the above emails are exaggerated a bit by a lonely or angry teen. However, it's important to also consider that maybe their parents *are* being stubborn and unfair to their teens, or that a sibling *is* being verbally or physically abusive.

There should be a hard and fast rule in every family that they will treat each other with respect—no exceptions, no excuses. It is never appropriate to get a laugh at someone else's expense—especially within a family. Every member of your family should feel safe and valued in your home.

Where Does Your Family Stand?

Ask yourself some hard questions and give an honest answer to each one:

- Is our home a place where my daughter is encouraged to share her opinions, preferences, and feelings, or is it more of a dictatorship where the parents are always right and not to be questioned?
- Does my daughter have my permission to discover who God created her uniquely to be, or do I think I know what's best for her and who she should become?
- Do I dictate which sports, activities, and clubs my daughter will be involved in?
- Do we have an open-door policy in our family? Is my daughter encouraged to come to me with any problem or concern without fear of being put down or laughed at?
- Do I have a favorite child whom I treat differently from the rest?

- Does my daughter invite her friends into our home, or would she rather go to someone else's house that might not be so tense?
- Is our home relationally healthy, or are there secrets we keep from the outside world?
- Is physical, verbal, or emotional abuse tolerated in our home?
- Do we have unnecessary rules? Are there areas where we can flex a bit and still maintain our personal standards and boundaries?
- Is my daughter afraid to talk to me about personal issues? If so, why? What can I do to make it easier for her to come to me when she needs to talk to someone?

Our families shape who we are and what we think of ourselves. A healthy home where everyone is loved and treated equally will produce confident and emotionally stable children. On the other hand, dysfunctional homes produce insecure and angry children who tend to act out or become emotionally crippled adults.

Maybe you were one of those broken children who was not loved and nurtured when you were growing up. The *great* news is that you don't have to raise your children that way! You *can* break the mold and have a brand-new start with your own family. You don't have to limp along, crippled by your own damaged emotions due to a dysfunctional childhood home.

It may take some professional help, but unearthing painful memories can help you overcome your difficult past and become a better parent to your daughter.

Chapter 8

"About Dad . . ."

✉ My dad has never told me he loves me! He's never hugged me, and it just hurts so bad! I see my friends' dads treating them special and talking with them, and it makes me cry. I want that so much! Why doesn't he love me?

✉ My mom never talks about my dad, and I haven't seen him since I was a baby. I don't have any idea who he is and I don't know anything about him. I don't know how to tell my mom I want to see him. I don't want to hurt her, but I want to know what happened and why I don't get to have a dad.

✉ My dad tries to be cool in front of my friends, and in doing so he always ends up embarrassing me. I don't want to hurt his feelings and tell him I'm embarrassed to be with him in public, but his jokes and attempts to act cool are backfiring big time!

✉ My mom and dad divorced when I was two years old. My dad had an affair, and I don't know if I can ever forgive him for that. He never calls just to talk with my sister or me. Once when he did call, it was to tell us he had another child. When he called that time, it was the day before my birthday, and he didn't even mention it! That really hurt.

I recently found out that he now has four children. I'd like to see him more often, and I even want to learn how to forgive him, but how?

✉ Every time I look at my dad, I'm reminded of an incident I learned about between him and one of his female co-workers. It involved Internet porn. I want to forgive him, but I can't forget about it. What can I do?

✉ My dad and I don't have a good relationship. He gets along great with my sister and brother, but it's a different story with me. I've tried desperately to have a relationship with him, but nothing has worked. I think this is affecting my relationship with all guys.

✉ I get really uncomfortable when my dad looks at me. So I'm wondering . . . can a dad get physically aroused by seeing his daughter in a swimsuit or tight shirt?

✉ My dad's always hugging on me and kissing me. I'm sick of it! I'm not ten anymore. How do I let him know I don't like it anymore? He's acting as though I'm still a little girl.

✉ My dad thinks everyone else is wrong, and he's always right. If someone in my family tries to correct him, he yells at us. He always complains about how disrespectful we are and how we don't appreciate anything. It hurts. Why is he so stubborn?

✉ My dad says he's a Christian, but he gets really angry sometimes and loses control. He's mean to my little sister. Last night I heard him screaming at her, and she really didn't do anything wrong. He kicked her across the room, and now she has a huge bruise. He even said that if my mom died, he'd kill my sister—that's how mad he was. My mom said that if it weren't for us children, they'd probably be divorced.

✉ To say my dad and I don't get along is an understatement! He gets mad at the smallest things. For instance, he yells at me and says I'm drinking too much apple juice, or he gets angry if I forget to put my socks away. I think he could definitely tell me things in a nicer way, but when he doesn't, I just can't seem to hold my tongue, and then he calls me disrespectful. I know the Bible says to obey and respect your parents, but it's really tough! What should I do?

✉ Sometimes I wish I could run away from home and never look back. My dad's not a Christian. He cusses, and he's almost always drunk. I just watched him going down the hallway, and he could barely walk. He disgusts me! He won't even talk or listen about God.

✉ Any interaction I have with my dad is very uncomfortable. I don't have much respect for him; we can't even have a normal conversation. He's so rude and abrupt. I've apologized to him because I know it takes two, but things were only better for about a week. Do you think God has stopped answering my prayers because I disrespect my dad?

✉ Because my mom and dad are divorced, I have to travel across the state to see Dad twice a month. I hate it. He never acts like he wants to see me, and the apartment he's in is really dumpy and gross. I'd rather not visit him anymore.

✉ My dad never has time for our family. He works so hard that we never get to play games or just hang out together like other families. He's working extra hours so we can buy a new car, but I'd much rather have my dad spend time with me than have a new car.

I keep thinking that I'll soon be grown, and I won't be around any longer. Won't he miss me?

✉ I don't think my dad cares about anything except himself. He's rude and moody and never asks any of the rest of us what we want to do or where we want to go; it's always his choice. It's gotten to where I don't want to go anywhere with my family. It's just no fun. I have to live with him four more years before I can leave home.

✉ My dad's a deacon in the church and while there, he acts like the perfect Christian. But at home he's a completely different person. He yells at my mom and treats my brothers and me like we're always in his way. Doesn't God hate hypocrites?

✉ My dad died a couple of years ago, leaving my mom, my sister, and me alone. I miss him so much. He was a good daddy. I know he loved me, but I can't help but be angry that he left us. My mom is now in a dating relationship with a guy I don't like, and I'm afraid she'll marry him. He'll never be my dad.

✉ I'm fourteen, and my dad died when I was ten. My mom has remarried, and I love my stepdad and my new brothers and sister. Would it be wrong to call him Dad? I get frustrated because I want to, but when I do it feels wrong. And when I don't, it feels wrong. What do I do? Is it wrong to call someone else Dad?

Every young girl dreams of her wedding day and the handsome guy she'll marry—her Prince Charming. Sadly, many of the girls who wrote these emails have lost the dream of ever finding a husband who will love and cherish her like the storybooks say.

They've lost their respect for men because the man in their young lives—their father—has let them down. Their hopes of "happily ever after" dashed, some don't want to marry at all if it's going to be anything like what they see at home.

These men have no idea the power their behavior has on their young daughters' tender hearts. Being loved or not loved by her father shapes the way a young girl sees herself and men in general. It can also shape how she sees God—her heavenly Father.

If her earthly dad is gruff and unloving, she sees God the same way. If he's mean and heartless, God must be too. If he's undependable and never keeps his word, God must be the same. If he mistreats his wife, why would his daughter ever want to get married?

Fathers have a huge responsibility to model Christlike behavior to their families. Jesus modeled leading by serving. He was tender and compassionate, yet strong and unwavering, never inconsistent. He treated women with respect, elevating them to a higher social standing than the culture of the day allowed. He taught His followers by example.

There are no perfect families, but we've seen the difference between those that are led by a godly, loving man and those that aren't. It's sobering.

It's ironic. There are many non-Christian men who are *wonderful* fathers who love and nurture their families so beautifully. Then there are many who claim to be followers of Christ but who also, for one reason or another, are broken men who don't know *how* to love their families.

What we want these hurting and disillusioned daughters to know is that no matter how disappointing their earthly fathers may be, they have a *heavenly Father* who's crazy about them and will move heaven and earth if He has to just to draw them to himself.

If you know a young girl who has never known Daddy's love the way God intended her to know it—the way she hungers for it—she needs to be introduced to her heavenly Father, who will never leave her or mistreat her. You could be the one to bring healing to a damaged young heart.

Bring It Home

What about your own daughter? Do you see a sadness in her that comes from a "dad-shaped hole" in her heart? If you do, prayerfully ask God to show you how to bridge the gap between her and her dad. If he's still in the home, he may not even realize what his emotional detachment is doing to his daughter.

If he's not in the home and your daughter rarely sees him, reassure her that not all men break the hearts of those who love them. Most important, assure her that God, her heavenly Father, will never abandon her. Try memorizing Hebrews 13:5 together, and say it often: "Keep your lives free from the love of money and be content with what you have, because God has said, 'Never will I leave you; never will I forsake you.' "

Being abandoned or mistreated by her father leaves a deep scar in a young girl's heart. He's supposed to be her protector, the one who provides for her physical and emotional needs.

How a young girl relates to her father will directly shape how she feels about men in general. If her father left her and the family for another woman, it can be difficult to trust any man who pledges his love for her. In the back of her mind she may battle thoughts such as *He's gonna leave you too* or *You'll never be good enough to keep his attention. You need to be thinner, smarter, prettier. You'll never measure up.*

Mom, you can play an important role in helping your daughter cope with abandonment issues when there's no father in the home. How? By *your* attitude toward him.

Ask yourself these questions:

- *Do I bad-mouth her father, portraying him as a loser, a drunk, or a no-good jerk?* If so, STOP! You're only making her pain worse. Try instead to give her *something* positive about him to hang on to, even if only in her dreams.
- *Do I verbally blame all our problems and financial woes on him?* How does that help her? Find an adult friend to whom you can vent your frustrations; don't take it out on your children. It's not their fault.
- *Does my daughter know the divorce/abandonment was not her fault?* You may assume she knows that, but kids have a way of internalizing blame for causing their parents to fight. Even if her father just couldn't deal with the responsibility of parenthood, she needs to hear from you that it was *his* problem, not hers. Tell her so.

Don't be afraid to seek help from a pastor or professional Christian counselor who can help your hurting daughter deal with the pain that comes from the lack of a healthy father figure in her life. Dealing with this loss when she's young will save years of heartache down the road and may even save her future marriage.

Quality Dads

It doesn't take a rocket scientist to become a good dad. If your husband *is* in the home, encourage him that *anything* positive he does will be an encouragement to your daughter. She may not acknowledge it, and he may not realize how important the small things can be, but even his *small* actions can make a difference.

Here are some ways my (Susie's) dad has made (and is still making) a difference in my life:

- *He's proud of me*. I know, because he tells me often. He told me as a little girl, and he still tells me as an adult. Hardly a phone call ends between us that he doesn't say, "Oh, Susie! I'm so proud of you. God is faithful, isn't He!" I can't express the incredible security that gives me! To know Dad is proud of me gives me confidence and a desire to work hard.
- *He loves me*. I know, because he tells me *and* shows me often. He told me and showed me as a little girl, and he still tells me and shows me as an adult. Even today, as we talk long-distance, Dad always tells me he loves me. He says it, he writes it in cards, he sends it through emails. He goes overboard to make sure his daughter is aware of his great love. But it's not simply words. Dad has always *shown* me his love as well.

  Last year I moved into a new house, and eight months later, I still had a garage full of boxes. It was so full, I couldn't even drive my car inside. My dad—my eighty-three-year-old dad, who'd already had one knee replacement and was in line for another one—drove to Colorado for an extended weekend to rearrange, organize, and clean out my garage. I knew it would be hard. I begged him not to come. I couldn't stand the thought of him working so hard for me. "Dad, my travel schedule will eventually slow down," I said. "And when I can get a couple of weekends at home, I'll do it." But he knew my schedule and realized it would be a long while before the travel slowed.

  He worked, he cleaned, he organized, he built shelves, he rearranged, and when I got home from my next speaking engagement, my car was inside the garage! My heart melted. In fact, my eyes are filling with tears even now as I write about it. His back hurt, and his knees were swollen, but he was grinning from ear to ear. "We did it, honey. We got your car in." "No. *We* didn't do it, Dad. *You* did it. And it breaks my heart to know you've worked so hard. Why? Why did you do it? Why didn't you just let me wait? It would have eventually gotten done." "I did it, sweetie, because I love you. And I did it because I wanted you to be able to get your car in the garage before winter."

What a dad! Fathers often mistakenly think they need to do something expensive or important to show their daughters how much they love them. But guess what! It's through the everyday happenings, the boring chores of life, that Dad's love screams the loudest.

He has fun with me. My dad is a special combination. He's very detailed and smart, yet he's also creative and fun. (I picked up the creative, fun side from him, but unfortunately I didn't get his intelligence and organization.) He writes poetry, tells great jokes, and loves life, and people enjoy being around him. He taught me to swim, high jump, and play mini-golf. Neither of my parents made tons of money. They were both teachers on a limited budget, but they made sure we took a family vacation every summer. They knew the importance of having fun as a family, and they wanted my brother and me to see as much of the United States as possible. Many vacations involved camping, and sometimes we went to an amusement park, but we consistently took a two-week vacation every August. Having fun doesn't have to cost a lot of money, but it does cost time. Encourage your husband that he *can* institute an element of fun within your family. When I was growing up, Dad took us to McDonald's every Friday evening. It was an inexpensive way to have fun together as a family, and it gave my brother and me something to look forward to. Friday family nights were never expensive, but they were consistent. Sometimes after McDonald's, we'd go bowling, play mini-golf, or simply go home and watch TV together. Sometimes we'd make popcorn, play board games, or watch family movies. The key ingredients? We did it every Friday (consistency), and we did it as a family (togetherness). Think of some ways you can encourage your husband to take the lead in establishing some fun, inexpensive things your entire family can do together.

Chapter 9

"Please Trust Me"

✉ My mom always wants me to talk to her. She's so nosy! It bothers her when I'm in my room with the door shut. I'm not trying to hide anything—sometimes I just don't feel like talking and want to be alone. How can I tell her that without hurting her feelings?

✉ My mom and dad are way too overprotective. I can't even go to the store on our corner without asking them. I can't go to sleepovers, and I can't drive or have a boyfriend until I'm eighteen. I can't even go to a Christian concert by myself. If I happen to like a guy, my mom freaks out and does everything to keep me away from him.

We argue all the time, and she tells me I'm disrespectful and a gossiper. I spend most of my time locked in my room—it's just better that way.

✉ My parents are sooooo protective. They don't let me go anywhere without knowing every little detail about where I'll be, who I'll be with, when I'm coming home, even where we're going to eat! I'm seventeen years old, and I've never done anything to cause them not to trust me.

⌧ I'm thirteen, but you'd think I'm ten by the way my mom and dad treat me. They're way too strict! When my friends ask me to do something I immediately say no, because I know my parents won't let me. I realize they're trying to protect me, but it's really getting on my nerves.

⌧ Mom and Dad have never discussed dating with me. I'm sixteen and feel like they're simply avoiding this topic. I think they just don't want to face the fact that I'm growing up. They're being way too strict. It's like they never want me to have boys around for fear I might like one of them or something.

⌧ My mom and dad are always saying I should be more responsible, but how am I supposed to do that when they never let me out of their sight? It's like they don't trust me to do the right thing or make smart choices. I CAN if they'd just give me the chance!

⌧ I have a loud and pushy mother. She tries to dictate every part of my life—who my friends are, what I wear, where I go, everything. I can't have any friends that aren't Christians, because she's afraid they'll be a bad influence on me. I'm smart enough to know who to hang around with and who not to. I feel like I'm being smothered!

⌧ A couple of kids I know went to a party where there was drinking and got caught. Now my parents are paranoid about who my friends are and think I'll do something stupid too. I'd never do that! How can I get them to trust me? I don't do that kind of stuff, but they're afraid I might start.

✉ I messed up one time and missed my curfew by ten minutes. It really wasn't my fault, and I apologized to my mom, but now she doesn't trust me. How can I regain her trust? It was just a mistake.

✉ How can I get my parents to trust me? My older brother got in trouble and ended up in jail, and now they don't let me do anything. I think they're scared I'll turn out like him. I won't! I'm nothing like him! I wish they'd let me prove myself; I'm a good girl!

✉ I caught my mom snooping in my drawer and reading some notes my friends had written me at school. Now she thinks I do some of the things they do, but I don't. She won't even let me hang out with them anymore, and they're the only friends I have! Forget about her trusting me — I can't trust her! Why can't she give me a little space and stay out of my stuff?

✉ I think I'm going to explode! My mom has to know everything I do and say. It's driving me insane. I can't even talk to my friends on the phone without her asking me what we were talking about. I'm tired of all her questions.

Having their parents trust them is a *huge* issue with teenagers. Being able to trust your daughters is a *huge* issue with parents. How can you both win?

For all of us, having someone say they don't trust us is like a slap in the face, especially if we haven't done anything to make them *not* trust us. For teens, it can feel like they spend their entire life trying to prove to adults that they're good kids and deserve to be trusted.

No doubt about it, when our daughters become teens, where they go and who they're with aren't always in our control anymore, and that's a scary thing for parents to deal with. More than anything, our daughters are trying to show us how grown up they are and that we *can* trust them to make wise decisions.

Learning to be responsible is a process just like learning to walk. Your daughter may slip up now and then just like she did when she was learning to walk; but that doesn't mean she's not trustworthy. It may be that she simply had a lapse in judgment and wasn't watching the time when her curfew came and went.

It may have been something out of her control, such as a friend who was driving her and had to stop for gas on the way home. Try not to be too quick to judge until she's had a chance to explain.

There are times when the best way to learn is by our own mistakes. When your teen does make a mistake, use the opportunity to make it a learning experience, not a criminal offense. Most of the time, it only takes once and girls quickly learn they don't want to lose your trust in them.

What If I Really Don't Trust Her?

Repeat offenses are a sure sign that either you've given too much responsibility too soon or that your daughter doesn't appreciate the freedoms you've given her. In that instance, you may have to pull in the reins a bit until you see that she's ready to be more responsible. As she proves she can be trustworthy, she gains more freedom.

A good rule of thumb is to tell your daughter you'll trust her until she gives you a reason not to. If and when that happens, you may have to go back and start from the beginning and have her earn your trust again before more privileges are granted.

Our experience has been that most teenagers really are good kids and want their parents to trust them. Don't borrow trouble where there is none. Just because other teens mess up in this area doesn't mean your daughter will.

Obviously you can't expect a thirteen-year-old to have the judgment and maturity of a seventeen-year-old, or a seventeen-year-old the maturity of a twenty-four-year-old. Be careful not to expect too much from an inexperienced young girl.

Psychologists tell us that the part of the brain responsible for impulse control isn't fully developed until age twenty-five. Some of us *never* have full control of our impulsive behavior!

If you're having trust issues with your daughter, ask yourself these questions:

- Have you given your daughter too much freedom too soon—more than she can handle at her age?
- Do you expect more mature behavior than she's capable of?
- Are your expectations clear, or do you assume she should know better at her age?
- If she does mess up, do you hold it against her or give her a second chance to prove herself?

Sometimes it's not completely the teen's fault when there's miscommunication about curfews, boundaries, and expectations. Be sure you've made yourself clear when letting your daughter know what you expect of her in these areas.

Read the following cases. Who do you think is at fault? Also look for any similarities between the people below and yourself.

Case #1:

Gwendolyn grew up in a church home with a small youth group. Because there weren't many teens, her most important friendships were established at school. Gwendolyn professed to be a Christian; she went to church camp every summer, and she enjoyed reading her Bible. She even considered becoming a missionary.

When Gwendolyn reached dating age, guys from school took notice. There was only one guy her age at church, and he wasn't interested in her. So when guys from school began asking her out, Gwendolyn accepted. Many of the guys she went out with weren't Christians and didn't share her morality.

Gwendolyn maintained her high value system for about a year, but when Jake began pressuring her to go further physically, she caved in. He was a great guy, popular at school, great personality, and quarterback on the varsity football team. Gwendolyn felt special just to be dating him. It wasn't long until she gave her virginity to Jake—just so she could keep him interested.

You guessed it: Not long afterward, Jake found another girl, and Gwendolyn was heartbroken. She enrolled in a Christian college, began dating Christian guys, and eventually married Bryan, who was studying for ministry.

Gwendolyn and Bryan have been happily married for twenty years, but when their daughter reached age seventeen and was asked out by a guy at school, problems arose.

"She's not dating anyone who doesn't go to our church!" Gwendolyn announced to Bryan.

"But, honey, we *know* Ryan. We've known his family for years! They're great people. He's only asked to take her to the school basketball banquet."

"I don't care. He doesn't go to our church. I'm serious about this, Bryan! Our daughter is *not* dating anyone from school."

"Babe, I don't see the harm in allowing her to attend a school function with a guy we both know and like."

What's going on? Gwendolyn is taking her own mistakes and turning them into the fear that her daughter may follow suit. She's thinking, *That's when the trouble began for me! I let my guard down with a guy from school. and our daughter will probably do the same thing.*

- Instead of assuming her daughter will repeat Gwendolyn's mistakes, what kind of compromise could solve this dilemma?
- Who's responsible for the lack of trust in this mother-daughter relationship?

Case #2:

Chenelle knew her curfew was 11 p.m. She had begged her mom to expand the time to midnight but couldn't convince her to do so.

Chenelle and three girlfriends went out for pizza and then headed to the theater for a fun chick flick. The early evening show they planned on seeing was sold out, so they purchased tickets for the next show, which started at 8:30 p.m.

The girls giggled, munched on popcorn, and even shed a few tears during the movie. Chenelle glanced at her watch as they exited the theater: 10:30 p.m. *Great*, she thought. *Shouldn't have any problem getting home by eleven.*

Traffic, however, was horrendous. The roadblock the girls had to navigate around hadn't been there earlier in the evening. *I can't believe this!* Chenelle thought. *The streets are jammed and cars are moving at a snail's pace!*

When she finally got home, it was 11:40, and her mom was waiting on the couch.

- Who's responsible for breaking the trust between mom and daughter?
- Is there anything that Chenelle could have done to maintain her mom's trust while she was in the middle of a situation she couldn't control?
- What would be an appropriate response for Mom? For Chenelle?

Case #3:

Jaime was a good girl; she just easily lost track of time. That's probably because she was such a people person. She was a great listener, and others usually shared their problems with her. Jaime gave good advice, and she was trusted among her peers.

She valued her friendships and always sought opportunities to get together. Jaime knew her curfew was midnight, but sometimes she was so involved in helping a friend that she simply didn't think to watch the clock.

Marcie understood her daughter's personality and admired Jaime's people skills, but she also talked seriously with her about the importance of remembering to check her watch and to be cognizant of the time. When Jaime didn't make curfew, she didn't miss it by much, but she *did* miss it a few times.

While not wanting to lessen her involvement with good friends, Marcie *did* want Jaime to know her curfew was a serious rule. "The next time you're late," she announced to her daughter, "you'll be grounded for a week."

Jaime couldn't stand the thought of not going out with her friends for a whole week, so when she drove to Abbie's house on Saturday evening, she made sure she was wearing her watch. The girls baked cookies, talked about guys, shared secrets, watched a movie, and pulled a few pranks on Abbie's little brother.

Jaime was having so much fun, she forgot to check her watch until she heard the grandfather clock in Abbie's hallway chime midnight. *Oh, no!* she thought. *I'm already late. And the drive home is at least twenty minutes.*

She climbed into the car and drove straight home, thankful to see that the house lights were out and her parents were already in bed.

The next morning, Jaime dressed for church and went downstairs for breakfast. Her family was already eating muffins and cereal when she approached the table. "Honey, did you make curfew last night?" Marcie asked.

"Mom! Are you serious? I don't want to be grounded! Believe me, I know how important curfew is!"

Jaime filled her bowl with cereal and read the cartoon section of the Sunday paper while her mom cleared the table and announced they'd be leaving for church in five minutes.

Wow. That was close! Jaime thought.

What Jaime didn't know was that while her mom was in bed when Jaime came home, she wasn't asleep. She had turned to the clock on her nightstand when she heard Jaime come through the front door at 12:25.

- What kind of trust issues will develop between Marcie and Jaime because of Jaime's response to her mom's question regarding curfew?
- Who's to blame for the unraveling of trust between the two?
- Can this relationship be strengthened? If so, how?

Set the Example

Moms, have you read our first book, *Here for You: Creating a Mother-Daughter Bond That Lasts a Lifetime*? If you haven't, will you consider doing so? It talks about the importance of making a mother-daughter covenant. There are five parts of the mother's covenant to her daughter, and there are five parts of the daughter's covenant to her mom. One piece of the daughter's oath to her mom is *I will always be honest with you.*

If Jaime had made such a covenant with her mom, it may have deterred her from being deceitful. Moms, no doubt you desire your daughter's honesty, but are you willing to set the example?

Does she see you being deceptive to your husband about the way you spend money or "adjust" the family budget? When it's time to turn in your tax report, does she notice you hiding a few items that the government probably won't catch?

Honesty, trust, and integrity are all part of character. What kind of character are you displaying for your daughter? Hopefully, you're living out Ephesians 5:1, which tells us to imitate our heavenly Father. If you're copying the lifestyle of Christ, you're being honest and trustworthy with your daughter. And in return, you can expect the same of her. Let her learn by your example.

Chapter 10

Cutting and Eating Disorders

Cutting

✉ I cut myself once, and I felt so bad about it, I promised God I'd never do it again. It's supposed to be His battle now, not mine. But I still struggle, especially when I'm depressed. Sometimes I just want to feel pain so bad! I'd rather have physical pain to deal with than the mental abstract fog they call depression.

✉ Why is self-harm wrong? I've done it before and sometimes still do, but everyone flips out. Hey, yelling at me is not going to help! Thanks, Mom, but I already know I'm a failure.

✉ About cutting: I don't understand what the big deal is. Sure, I'll have to keep those scars, but I don't care. The guy I'll marry someday gets the whole package — scars, mistakes, looks, hurts, heart, and all.

✉ Self-harm is a form of stress relief or punishment on yourself. I think it's okay. It's not like it's a sin.

✉ I've grown up in a Christian home, but a few years ago I turned away from God. My mom is a Sunday school teacher and is really involved in the church. It got to the point where she was too busy for me or any of my problems. I started cutting in the tenth grade, and finally during my senior year, I told my small-group leader. She made me tell my mom.

My mom wouldn't even talk to me about it. She just made me see a Christian counselor who was very loving and helpful. But my mom kept asking me if I was all better yet, and I felt like all she was concerned about was that I was ruining her good reputation. Mom finally told me that counseling was too expensive, and she didn't feel like paying for it anymore, so I had to stop going even though I wasn't ready to quit. So I've never really stopped cutting. Now I feel I'm right back where I started.

✉ My youth group recently went on a retreat, and I gave my life to Christ. But I have a problem with cutting — it's very calming. I want to stop, but I can't find a substitute for it.

✉ I started cutting myself last summer. I really want to stop but I can't. One of my best friends is a cutter too, but the difference is she always encourages it, and I want to stop. I know I should go to God first, but that just doesn't seem possible. I've fallen so far away from Him. I just don't know what to do.

✉ I'm a hypocrite, and I know it. I live two different lives. I wear a mask when I'm around people and act like life is wonderful. The me that no one knows struggles with an eating disorder, cuts herself all over her body, and does anything possible to numb the pain of being me.

✉ I was diagnosed with depression a year ago. I started cutting myself but was able to hide it for several months. Then my mom found out and made me quit. Lately my family's been fighting a lot, and it's made me fall back into that depression. Now I want to start cutting again.

☒ I had a problem with cutting about two years go. One of my friends told our school counselor, and he got me help. I've been having a really hard time with stress. About a week ago I broke down and cut myself again. I don't want to tell anyone — they'll be so disappointed in me.

☒ A few years ago my mom and dad got a divorce. After the initial shock wore off; I found a way to deal with it. I started listening to goth music and cried alone at night on my pillow. Shortly after I bought the My Chemical Romance CD, I began cutting myself because I enjoyed watching the blood trickle down my arm, and I hoped someone would notice my pain. I feel incredibly empty inside. I'm so emotionally exhausted and alone.

☒ Don't tell me to talk to my parents! If I could tell them what's going on in my life, I wouldn't be writing you. I want to tell my parents that I'm a former cutter, have dreams of suicide, and haven't eaten more than one meal a day in the past month! I want to talk to my mom, but I just can't.

☒ My life is spinning out of control! My family doesn't understand me. I get yelled at almost every day, and I cry all the time. I have a lot of stomach pains and headaches, and I've been extremely depressed and tired. I'm beginning to wonder if God really has a plan for my life . . . and even if He really exists.

You may not even see it coming. Your busy family goes their separate ways every day and you may not see that much of each other in the evenings. With homework, ball games, PTA meetings, church board meetings, and baby-sitting jobs, life is crazy!

Things seem to be going along just fine. Your daughter appears to be happy and doing okay in school. Sure, there are the usual mood swings, but that's normal teen behavior.

Then it hits you right in the gut. It comes out of nowhere—that phone call from the school counselor informing you that your daughter has been hurting herself.

"Self-mutilating," they call it. Your head spins and a wave of nausea hits you hard. What in the world is *that*? There must be some mistake. *"Not MY daughter. She's the president of her church youth group! She's a good kid!"*

Even good, churchgoing teens fall into the trap of self-injury, often called "cutting." It's been described as this generation's eating disorder (though eating disorders are still widespread). Girls *and* guys self-mutilate, but it's more common among girls.

Cutting is a form of self-injury where kids will use any sharp object to slice their skin and watch themselves bleed. Although some use razor blades, knives, or scissors, others use thumbtacks, pins, staples, pens, fingernails, or barrettes. Still others will burn themselves with matches or a curling iron.

"Why would anyone want to do that?" you ask. It's a strange phenomenon that has hit our youth in epidemic proportions.

The majority of self-mutilators are Caucasian teen girls or young adult women who come from middle-class or upper-middle-class families. Some, though, start as young as middle school.

Often this behavior goes unnoticed, as scratched and scarred arms and legs are hidden under long-sleeved shirts and long pants. Some cleverly cut in the stomach area, where it can't be seen by others.

Why Cut?

Ask a teen girl who cuts herself why she does it and she'll probably say things like, "It's a release of stress and feels good," or "It's the only thing in my life I truly have control over." Often it's, "My emotional pain is so deep that I feel dead. When I cut myself and see the blood dripping down my arm, at least I know I'm alive."

One thirteen-year-old said, "I started cutting myself as a way of coping. I was holding everything inside, so I started venting with razors."

They're not trying to kill themselves; instead, cutters see their actions as a way of handling their emotions without hurting anyone else. *No one else even has to know*, they reason. It's a private way of coping.

For most, self-injury is a way of expressing deep emotions they can't put into words. For others, it's a way of expressing anger—they feel better taking it out on themselves than hurting others. And some teens use it as a way of getting attention from people in their lives who will offer them comfort because of it.

What Are the Warning Signs?

Because this form of self-destructive behavior is done in secret, it may be difficult to know if your daughter is cutting herself. Watch for scars or scratches on her arms or legs if you suspect she may be self-injuring. Also note what she's wearing. If she consistently wears long-sleeved tops and long pants in hot weather, you have reason to be suspicious. Look for sharp objects in her room or bathroom that typically don't belong there such as razors, pieces of glass, or bent paper clips.

Know that self-injury is always a symptom of a deeper emotional problem. Simply demanding she stop won't fix things.

Often it's a problem dealing with emotions that are held in and not expressed appropriately.

If you suspect your daughter is cutting herself, realize that this problem is much bigger than the two of you. Seek the help of a professional counselor who can evaluate her motives for cutting and help her develop healthy ways of coping with her stress.

For an inside peek from a teen girl who battled cutting, turn to appendix A.

Eating Disorders

✉ I'm twelve years old, a little more than five feet tall, and I weigh 143 pounds. I think I'm fat. My family and all my friends say I'm not. Mom says I have a lot of muscle. I often think about starving myself, but I know that's wrong.

✉ Okay. My mom was probably trying to be helpful, but a few months ago, she suggested I go on a diet and try eating more sensibly. Ever since then I've become paranoid. I'm skipping meals and only eating a small salad every day. I'm starting to lose weight—which thrills me—but I'm really hungry. I'm so hungry, I can't stop thinking about food! Do you think I've developed an eating disorder?

✉ I hate my body. Kids made fun of me in grade school for being chunky, so the summer before middle school, I decided to do something about it. I run six miles every morning, and I exercise each evening. My mom packs a lunch for me to take to school, but she doesn't know I just toss it in the garbage. I've lost some weight, but I still feel fat.

✉ I've been anorexic for about a year. I can't even take communion at church because I'm obsessed with how many calories are in the cracker. I want help, but I'm afraid if I get help, they'll make me gain weight!

✉ Nobody knows this, but I throw up three or four times a day. I heard you can lose weight this way. Now I think I'm addicted to it. And now if I don't throw up I feel sick.

More than three thousand young women die each year from complications resulting from eating disorders. Observation is key for parents to detect any kind of eating disorder.

We live in a culture where the message is screamed everywhere you turn: Thin is beautiful; the more thin, the more beautiful. As adults, we know this is hogwash, but our daughters tend to believe what they see and hear. And young girls who are desperate to look and feel beautiful like the models they see on magazine covers, in movies, and on TV don't know the difference between being healthy and slender, and dangerously underweight and obsessed with their calorie intake.

What is an eating disorder? Typically, it manifests itself in one of two ways—anorexia or bulimia.

Anorexia

Anorexia is when a person stops eating altogether, trying to starve herself thin, or she eats only tiny amounts of food each day—not enough to sustain a healthy body weight. The anorexic is obsessed with calorie intake and will often give the appearance of eating in front of others but then rush to the bathroom immediately to throw up what was just eaten. Another popular way to eliminate what was digested is the abuse of over-the-counter laxatives, which can lead to dehydration and digestive problems.

This dangerous aversion to food can result in many life-threatening health issues, including heart and organ failure

Typically, no matter how thin a girl with anorexia gets, she'll always see herself as fat when she looks in the mirror. Self-loathing consumes her thoughts—she hates what she sees. Food is her enemy.

But it's not really food that's the problem. There's always a deeper issue. For many girls, it's control. For some teens, anorexia is a way to control something in their lives when everything else seems out of control. What she puts into her body is the one thing no one else can control. It's a desperate cry for help covering a much deeper emotional need.

Warning Signs of Anorexia

- Anxiety about weight
- Preoccupation with food, calories, and dieting
- Pushing food around on the plate to give the impression of eating
- Excessive, rigid exercise routine
- Withdrawal from family and friends
- Depression
- Evidence of self-induced vomiting and/or laxative use
- Trips to the bathroom immediately following every meal
- Raw knuckles/broken blood vessels around eyes and nose

Bulimia

People with bulimia are bingers and purgers. Food is their best friend, whereas for someone with anorexia, food is the enemy.

People with bulimia seek comfort in food and may eat large quantities at a time to fill an emotional need. To keep their weight down, they will then head for a bathroom to throw up all they've ingested. Some people with bulimia will spend hundreds of dollars every week hopping from one fast-food spot to another to satisfy their cravings, only to purge as soon as they can to avoid gaining weight.

Many binge late at night when everyone else is in bed and can't see what they're doing. Abuse of laxatives is another way of expelling the food consumed.

Contrary to their goal, many people with bulimia maintain normal or above normal body weight, often hiding their problem for years. Binges and purges can range from once or twice a week to several times a day.

Warning Signs of Bulimia

- Obsessive thoughts of food or weight
- Evidence of vomiting
- Frequent trips to the bathroom following meals
- Evidence of laxative/diuretic use
- Secret eating/hoarding food or evidence of missing food
- Raw knuckles/broken blood vessels around eyes and nose

Severe cases of anorexia or bulimia often require hospitalization or treatment from a facility specializing in eating disorders where nutritional counseling, medication, and individual and family therapy are available.

Even with treatment, many patients with eating disorders struggle for the rest of their lives. It's a weak area that will often resurface during times of stress. However, it *is* possible to recover fully if the disorder is caught early and treatment is sought.

If you suspect your daughter may have an eating disorder, don't be afraid to confront her about it. Seek professional medical and psychological help immediately. The earlier an eating disorder is discovered and treated, the better the chances of her recovery.

For an inside peek at someone who has struggled with an eating disorder and is now experiencing victory, turn to appendix B.

How Can Parents Help Prevent Cutting and Eating Disorders?

The most effective way to prevent self-destructive behavior in your teens is to lead by example. Test yourself to see what kind of role model you are. Ask yourself:

- Do I handle emotions in a healthy way?
- Do I make myself available for my daughter to share her emotions?
- Do I constantly complain about my weight or make comments about feeling fat?
- Do I comment in a negative way on others who have put on weight?
- Do I take care of my body by proper diet and appropriate exercise?
- Have I told my daughter she'd look better if she'd just lose five pounds?

Your comments and behaviors don't go unnoticed by your daughter! What you model to her in your own life will speak louder than what you say.

If your daughter is caught cutting:

DON'T

- Condemn her. She already knows what she's doing isn't right.
- Point attention to the physical scars. She knows they're disgusting. Remember, those scars have come out of great pain. Your daughter doesn't know how to accept herself. She hates who she is.

DO

- Watch for warning signs. (Overly modest; not wanting to change in front of her friends, wearing shorts and a shirt over a swimsuit so no one will see the scars.)
- Ask her straight out if she's cutting or burning herself.
- Give her lots of hugs.
- Take her to get professional help from a Christian counselor or your pastor.

Excerpted from How to Help Your Hurting Friend *by Susie Shellenberger. Zondervan Publishing. Copyright 2003. Used with permission.*

Chapter 11

Drinking and Other Self-Destructive Behaviors

Alcohol and Drugs

✉ I live in a small town and there's absolutely nothing to do except drink. It's not like I planned to drink; it just happened. I've been doing it every week for almost a year now. Could I be an alcoholic?

✉ My life is a mess. Last year I was depressed and started cutting myself. I also got high on chemicals. Then I became a Christian, but drugs and gang lifestyle have a hard pull — especially the drugs. I thought I'd be free of that, but I'm back into snorting chemicals again, and my lifestyle isn't the best.

✉ I know most girls don't have problems with being part of gangs, but my whole town is gang territory, and a lot of the gangsters are my friends. I don't even know if I want to change. All I know is that the drugs are affecting my grades, and I've got to finish high school.

✉ I started drinking wine coolers because my friends said it wasn't like we were really drinking. After a while, I started drinking beer. I hated the taste, but everyone else was doing it, so I went along. Last night I got really drunk. I hate how I feel this morning. I don't want to drink anymore, but I don't know how to say no.

✉ A bunch of us were at a party, and someone was passing around pot. I'd heard all my life that drugs were wrong, but suddenly I couldn't remember why. So I smoked it. I liked how it made me forget about my family problems. I smoke it every chance I get. How can it be wrong if it makes me feel good about my life?

✉ I think I'm an alcoholic. I have to drink to even make it through the day. I mix alcohol with orange juice and fill my water bottle with it. No one knows, and I'm afraid to tell, but I need help.

Moms, if you keep alcohol in the house—even though it may be inside a locked cabinet—chances are your daughter is getting the message that drinking is okay. You may have explained that it's not okay for teens to drink—that it's illegal until age twenty-one—but if she sees you drinking, she's still going to interpret drinking as acceptable behavior.

We realize that Christians have a variety of opinions on drinking. We know, too, that Christ turned water into wine for His first miracle. And Paul encouraged Timothy to drink a little wine. But may we give you our personal belief? Neither of us drink. We're personally convicted against alcohol and just don't see any reason to partake of something that can so quickly lead to a downward spiral.

When Jesus turned water into wine, we have to remember that He didn't create a drunken orgy. Nor did He create Jack Daniel's. The wine Jesus created probably had such a tiny percentage of alcohol in it (for purification purposes), it wasn't even as strong as an American beer or a wine cooler.

And when the apostle Paul told his young minister friend Timothy to take some wine, it was for medicinal purposes; Timothy had a history of stomach problems. The Bible consistently warns against the abuse of alcohol.

Let's Look at the Facts

It's too bad that most teens don't see the connection between their actions today and the consequences they'll face in the future. Most teens feel indestructible and immune to the problems that others experience through alcohol and other drugs. Teens who use alcohol and tobacco are at a greater risk of using other drugs later.

One survey we found says that about 75 percent of high school students have tried alcohol. More alarming, about 28 percent of teens have had a recent episode of heavy drinking (more than five drinks within a couple of hours).

Do you realize that the leading cause of death for teens and young adults is auto accidents related to alcohol? As you know, drinking also lowers inhibitions, which can lead teens to have unprotected sex, increasing the chance of pregnancy and infection with sexually transmitted diseases, such as herpes, chlamydia, and HIV.

About 40 percent of teens have tried marijuana one or more times, while about 22 percent of teens currently use marijuana. Teen use is troubling because marijuana can hinder the memory, problem-solving abilities, and learning aptitude. It can also cause mood swings, anxiety, and depression.

About 9 percent of teens have tried cocaine, while 4 percent use it currently (one or more times in a month). Cocaine is an addictive drug. It's especially dangerous because it can cause abnormal heartbeats, occasionally resulting in a life-threatening heart attack, seizure, or stroke.

Why do teens use drugs? Why do they try alcohol? It's obvious from the emails we've shared that many are pressured into doing so. Others simply don't know how to say no. Some are simply curious, and others are desperately seeking an escape. Moms, this is why it's crucial that you talk openly and early with your daughter—not only about the dangers of alcohol and drug use, but also about how to establish boundaries for herself and stand against peer pressure.

There's really a deeper issue at stake, and that's the question of why your daughter wants to attend a party where alcohol and drugs will be present, or why she's interested in establishing close friendships with those who are involved.

Instead of simply reciting a volume of rules to her, strive to shape her heart. Remember, your goal as her mom is to help her fall deeply in love with Christ. This involves praying together, reading the Bible together, discussing everything from A to Z together, and seeking God's perspective.

Who's at Risk?

Teenagers at risk for developing serious alcohol and drug problems include those:

- with a family history of substance abuse. Studies indicate that when this genetic predisposition for abuse is combined with environmental factors, the person is more likely to develop a substance abuse problem.
- who are depressed. This may include chemical or emotional depression. Teens who struggle with depression

often experiment with drugs or alcohol in an attempt to feel "happy."

- who have low self-esteem. Teens from families with frequent conflict, physical or sexual abuse, or psychological stress usually struggle with a low self-esteem and are more likely to try alcohol and drugs. Without feelings of closeness, and with a poor self-image, a teen may look to alcohol or drugs to compensate for emotional pain.
- who feel as though they don't fit in or are out of the mainstream. Personal, family, and community factors increase a teen's risk for using substances and developing a substance abuse problem.
- who have certain diseases or conditions. Teens who have untreated attention deficit hyperactivity disorder (ADHD), conduct disorder, depression or long-term depressed feelings (dysthymia), post-traumatic stress disorder, or an anxiety disorder are more likely to use alcohol or drugs. Also, alcohol and drug abuse behaviors may worsen these conditions.
- who have drug expectations. A teen develops an expectation of what taking drugs or using alcohol will be like from parents, friends, and the media. Teens often have misconceptions about the harmful effects of alcohol, cigarettes, and drugs, and they often think that "everybody does it," and so should they.
- who use at an early age. Using alcohol or other drugs at a young age greatly increases a teen's risk for developing an abuse problem. One study found that teens who had their first alcoholic drink at age fourteen or younger were four to five times more likely to develop alcohol abuse problems than teens who had their first drink at age nineteen or older.

- who don't have much parental involvement. Lack of consistent parental involvement in a child's life and lack of appropriate supervision increase a teen's risk for abusing alcohol, cigarettes, and other drugs. Harsh or inconsistent punishment or permissiveness also increases a teen's risk for alcohol and drug abuse.

What to Look For

It can often be difficult to tell if your daughter is using alcohol or drugs. Parents may worry that their teens are involved with drugs or alcohol if they become withdrawn or negative, although these behaviors are common for teens going through challenging times. It's important that you not accuse her unfairly. Try to discover why her behavior has changed by telling her that you're concerned.

Most experts recommend that when alcohol or drug use is suspected, parents look for a pattern or a number of changes in appearance, behavior, and attitude, not only one or two changes. Substance abuse may be a possibility if several of the following signs are present:

- Less attention paid to dressing and grooming
- Loss of appetite or unexplained weight loss
- Red and glassy eyes and frequent use of eyedrops and breath mints
- Decreased attendance and performance at school
- Loss of interest in school, sports, or other activities
- Newly developed secrecy; deceptive or sneaky behavior
- Withdrawal from family and friends
- New friends and reluctance to introduce them
- Lying or stealing

- Disrespectful behavior
- A worsening mood or attitude
- Lack of concern about the future

Again, don't assume your daughter is using drugs or alcohol if one or two of these signs are present. And many of these signs would also be present for depression, cutting, or an eating disorder. Establish an honest relationship with your daughter early on so she feels comfortable in sharing her struggles with you—regardless of what they are. If your daughter exhibits several of these symptoms, you'll want to consider professional Christian counseling for her.

The Fainting Game

Searching for an inexpensive and ultimate high, children as young as nine and ten years old have dabbled in the deadly game called "the fainting game," "the passing out game," or "the choking game."

This is where they allow their friends to choke or hang them to cut off their air supply, causing a lack of oxygen to the brain. They're hoping to achieve a "buzz" similar to drinking or taking drugs. Sadly, children don't realize how dangerous this bizarre game really is. Instead of experiencing the desired high, many end up accidentally committing suicide.

The Internet draws many young people into the "game," often touting it to kids as "the best feeling ever."

Peer pressure is another reason kids are engaging in this dangerous behavior. They'll often take a dare or do anything to fit in or be considered cool.

Although boys more than girls participate in these deadly games, they've become a popular event at many teen parties.

Even college students find this a great way to get a good laugh as they watch the victim twitch and pass out as they let themselves be strangled.

What to Look For

The warning signs for the fainting game aren't as clear as those for experimenting with drugs or alcohol. Some may express interest in strangulation or ask questions about what happens when someone chokes.

Your daughter may seem groggy or unusually tired after coming out of her room with friends. Other warning signs would be suspicious marks on her neck, changes in her personality or behavior, or unusual items found in her bedroom such as scarves, belts, or rope. Headaches, a flushed face, a raspy throat, and bloodshot eyes are also warning signs of the fainting game.

Other Names of the Game

- Breath play
- Bagging
- Choking game
- Suffocation roulette
- Blackout
- Space monkey
- Knockout
- Airplaning
- Flat-liner
- Dream game
- Tingling game
- Funky chicken

Possible Injuries From the Game

- Concussion
- Broken jaw
- Fractured shoulders, ribs, or limbs
- Throat and voice injuries
- Accidental death

Teen Gambling

Even though legal gambling is restricted to those over eighteen years of age, an increasing number of teen girls have become addicted gamblers.

Studies done by the Council on Compulsive Gambling of New Jersey, Inc., indicate that gambling is on virtually every high school campus in America. When you get to the college level, it's epidemic. Gambling is also readily available to teens through the Internet.

This self-destructive behavior isn't as easy to spot as others, but there are warning signs that your daughter may have fallen victim to it. What starts out as an innocent game of chance can quickly draw teens into a lifelong addiction.

For teens, it typically starts with gambling on high school sports. It's not uncommon for students in junior and senior high schools to have a bookie, who gives them the opportunity to gamble on bigger games illegally and offers credit. It might start with a credit line of $25 or $50 a game. Kids can bet on games all week, and on Sunday night they tally up the money they made or owe.

The appetite is quickly formed for bigger stakes, and just like in the movies, bookies can get violent, starting with verbal abuse and threats if the teen doesn't pay up.

Gambling debt often leads to petty theft, which can eventually lead to more serious crimes like break-ins and selling drugs.

Although gambling is more common among teen guys than girls, there are warning signs parents should be aware of.

Signs of Teen Gambling

- Financial problems
- Schoolwork slides
- Missed classes at school
- Lack of focus
- Secretive behavior
- College students drop out without telling parents
- Emotional high followed by a downward spiral leading to desperation

Teen Smoking

The American Lung Association estimates that every day, six thousand children under eighteen will take their first drag off a cigarette. Of those six thousand, about two thousand will go on to be regular smokers. The fact that teen smoking rates are steadily increasing is disturbing. About 90 percent of adult smokers started smoking before age twenty-one.*

In spite of scientific evidence proving the health risks associated with cigarettes and other tobacco use, nearly three

**www.lungusa.org/site/apps/s/content.asp?c=dvLUK9O0E&b=34706&ct=66721.*

thousand teenagers take up the habit every day in the U.S. alone.

Twenty-first-century teens are smart. You may wonder what would drive them to make such an unhealthy life choice. To put it simply, for most, it's the need to fit in.

Taking up smoking is one way vulnerable adolescents can feel older and "wiser" than they really are. For others, it's an attempt to belong. The smokers huddle together in designated areas that become their hangout—their place to congregate, converse, and become a "family" of sorts.

For some, it's a way to act dangerous—the forbidden is alluring. The idea of breaking the law or going against their parents' wishes is for some as addicting as the nicotine itself.

Highly addictive nicotine acts as a stimulant to the mind, body, and spirit. If you suspect your daughter may be hiding a smoking habit, here are some common characteristics of teen smokers:

- They tried their first cigarette in sixth or seventh grade
- They often do not perform well in school
- They feel like they are not a part of the school
- They become isolated from other students
- They can't perform as well in sports
- They feel like they have little hope of going to college
- They are reported to school officials for skipping classes
- They start using other illegal substances
- They begin experimenting with alcohol and other drugs
- They experience pressure from home and school and use tobacco as a form of relief

- They feel like they need a job to support their smoking habit

How Can Parents Help Prevent Self-Destructive Behavior?

The most effective way to prevent self-destructive behavior in your daughter is to lead by example. Are you a good role model, or is your motto "Do as I say, not as I do"?

If you use or abuse tobacco, drugs, or alcohol, chances are greater that your daughter will emulate your behavior.

If you dabble in gambling, buying lottery tickets, placing friendly bets on sporting events, your actions condone these activities for your daughter as well.

Know that pressure to conform is a battle teens face every day.

Be aware of who your daughter's friends are and what they do for fun. Encourage her to participate in school and youth group activities. A strong self-esteem and busy schedule will go a long way in preventing her from falling into the trap of self-destructive behaviors.

Chapter 12

What Moms Are Afraid Of

Parenting teen girls in the twenty-first century is a challenge! Too many negative outside influences rob our daughters of innocence at an early age. As a result, many moms and dads parent out of fear and overreact simply because they don't want their daughters to be hurt.

Did you know the Bible says "Fear not" 365 different times? That's a "fear not" for every day of the year! And this applies to all areas of life—even parenting!

Here are some comments we've heard from moms and the fears they have as their daughters become teens.

> ✉ My heart is breaking for my fourteen-year-old daughter. The latest fad among her Christian friends is "burning"—social bullying and teasing where everything you say is twisted and turned into a joke. She's pleaded for them to stop, but they haven't, and they have no regard for her feelings. I tell her to simply ignore it or walk away, but that doesn't take away the hurt. I'm so afraid

this cruel treatment will turn her inward and she'll become socially depressed. Why are girls so cruel to one another?

✉ I have a sixteen-year-old daughter, and I'm terrified she'll make a mistake and ruin her life. I don't know how to talk to her about my fear without offending her and making her think I don't trust her.

✉ My daughter is a freshman in college. She's always been involved in our church denomination, but now that she's away from home she's trying out other faiths. I'm so afraid she'll reject the faith we raised her with and be swept into something we don't believe in. What if we didn't do enough while she was home to keep her from straying away from the church now that she's on her own?

✉ Can I sneak inside this book for a second? I don't have any daughters; I'm a mom of three teenage sons — and I'd like to offer some insight on what teen girls are wearing. Young girls think they look cute in short skirts, tight jeans, and see-through shirts, but they don't realize what teen boys (my sons) see when they look at them. When they look at your daughters, they don't see a little girl — they see a young woman!

I want my sons to stay pure in their thoughts. Please tell your daughters to help Christian young men stay pure by not dressing so provocatively. They can't help but look!

✉ Being a Christian parent is just as hard these days as being a Christian teen. I've been trying to teach my daughters how to guard their hearts as they go through life and to wait for the young man God has for them. Sometimes I wonder if I'm the only mom talking to her daughters about these kinds of things.

✉ My daughter will be going to a new high school next year, and I'm scared she'll fall into the wrong group of friends just to belong. She's a follower, not a leader. What can I do to help her find the right kinds of friends?

✉ I have two stepdaughters — twelve and fourteen — and I really struggle to communicate with them. These girls think the world revolves around their mom, and here I am — the stepmom — trying to teach them about God and right from wrong. When they spend weekends with their mom, it's like everything I've tried to teach them goes right out the window. I've caught them writing letters to their mom asking if they can live with her to get out of our house.

✉ I know it's normal for teen girls to want to be with their friends more than family, but I'm having a really hard time letting my daughter go. I don't want to smother her, but at the same time I'm afraid I'm losing her. She spends more time on the phone with her friends or going to the mall with them than she does with our family. How can I keep from losing her?

✉ My daughter used to come home from school and chatter on and on about her day and what her friends did. Sometimes I wanted to ask her to stop talking so much! Now that she's in middle school, she comes home and won't tell me anything! I feel as though I have to pull teeth to get her involved in a simple conversation. If I didn't keep asking questions, I'd never know what's going on in her life. I wish things were like they used to be.

✉ I thought my daughter and I would grow closer as she got older, but it's just the opposite. We don't communicate, she's rarely home when I am, and when we're both in the house, she's in her room on the phone or IMing with her friends. How can I stay connected with her when she shuts me out like that?

✉ I'm at a loss as to what to do with my seventeen-year-old daughter. She's moody, distant, and irritable. I just don't like her very much these days. Our entire family has to tiptoe around her moods. Any suggestions for us?

Kathy here:

I wish I could bring you all into my family room in Colorado today. I'd have us all sit down with a nice hot latte by the fireplace, where we could enjoy the view of the beautiful snow-covered Rocky Mountains—no cell phones, no husbands, no kids—just us moms having a heart-to-heart together. (So jump inside this heart-to-heart with me, okay? Go grab your favorite drink and meet me back here in ten minutes. I'll wait right here for you.)

My husband, Jeff, and I have been married nearly thirty years and have raised two kids—one who is a *very* emotional daughter.

Let me tell you some wonderful news: The hormonal teen years are TEMPORARY!

The truth is, moms, it's a different day than when we were teens, isn't it? We live in a culture that's out to destroy our daughters.

The media is feeding them lies that scream they're not good enough, not pretty enough, not thin enough, not smart enough . . . they'll never measure up. That's a lot of pressure that can leave our daughters feeling hopeless and completely alone.

My kids are now wonderful young adults. We made it through the teen years relatively sane, but let me tell you, *there were times when we wondered if we were going to make it without going completely crazy.*

I clearly remember telling Jeff that I really thought our daughter, Kelly, hated me. I HONESTLY DID!

It seemed as if no matter what I did or how hard I tried, we weren't on the same page about anything.

She'd barely talk to me, and when she did, it was often in an emotional outburst, yet I'd see her laughing and giggling with her friends' moms at church. *That hurt!*

I couldn't figure out what I was doing wrong and what they were doing right! I felt like a complete failure as a mom.

Then it hit me what the problem was: **I was her mother and they weren't!** That's all I was guilty of!

Remember When?

Reminisce with me for a moment. . . .

Remember when you first found out that your precious baby was a sweet little *girl*?

You dreamed and fantasized about how you would dress her in adorable outfits, put bows in her hair, and be best friends. You just knew you'd love to shop together and you'd teach her how to cook, and oh, how you'd laugh and have fun!

Oh, how you *loved* those days of snuggling a freshly bathed and powdered little bundle in her jammies! She cried when you left and was thrilled when you returned.

Remember those days?

Before you knew it, though, she started school, and your joy turned to fear.

Would she have anybody to sit by at lunch?

Would the other kids be nice to her?

Would her teacher hurt her feelings?

And just when you've adjusted to that phase—clipping along, enjoying being a room mother, helping with school parties, and having her *beg* you to go on her school field trips—she's entered middle school and suddenly acts as though she doesn't know you.

She doesn't want you to be involved.

In fact, she may even ask you to drop her off at the corner and she'll walk the rest of the way to school so as not to be seen with you! That was my daughter, Kelly. Her brother liked it when I dropped him off at the curb in front of his school and would even give me a kiss and a hug in front of his friends!

Not Kelly!

She was the one who wanted me to leave her at the corner so no one would see me.

I understand your fears.

It's like you woke up one day to find that someone broke into your home and took your sweet little girl and replaced her with an eye-rolling, door-slamming stranger on an emotional roller coaster!

You find yourself walking around on eggshells.

Your stomach is in knots as she comes in the door from school; what will it be today?

You don't know if she'll come home smiling and bouncy or cranky and irritable. It's as if you're held captive in your own home!

Your day is directly affected by *hers*. In fact, the whole family's day may be affected by hers.

What on Earth Happened?

I remember days when Kelly would get off the school bus and run into the house, slam the door, and burst into tears.

I thought someone must have died, only to find out her best friend sat by someone else at lunch that day!

All through her middle school years I never knew what to expect on any given day. It was horrible!

Don't laugh. If you haven't been there yet, you *will* be.

Suddenly your daughter's no longer talking to you. Instead, she's spending hours in her room talking on the phone and IMing with her friends behind closed doors.

Just when you think you might have a chance for a little conversation, she gets a text message from someone and has to respond immediately.

You've suddenly taken a backseat in her life.

When she *does* talk to you, it's short, sarcastic answers and sharp looks that leave you feeling like you're suddenly the dumbest person on the planet. You're left wondering how you got so ignorant.

It's a frightening and frustrating time for moms.

The truth is, it's also a difficult time for her.

She's in the midst of a metamorphosis.

Her "hors are moaning," if you know what I mean, and her body is changing faster than she can keep up with. I know you've heard it: "My feet are too big!" or "Why did I get this stupid hair!"

"Nothing looks good on me. I'm too skinny/too fat/too short."

She may be an early bloomer or a late bloomer—either one can feel like a curse for a young girl!

The jeans that fit yesterday don't fit today, one breast is bigger than the other, and her face is breaking out all over.

She's trying to figure out who she is.

Where does she fit in?

What is she good at?

Will she measure up?

She's dealing with expectations from parents, teachers, coaches, and friends.

She's *desperately* trying to fit in and be accepted. Worst of all, she may feel *invisible*.

To add to the drama, *your* hors are moaning, and your life is filled with fear:

- What if something bad happens to her? You panic every time she's five minutes late, and you make her promise to call you as soon as she gets to her friend's house.
- You begin to see that her friends have more control over her than you do.
- You feel as if you don't know what's going on in her life.
- She's irritable and moody. *You're* irritable and moody. Heaven forbid you end up on the same monthly cycle! The rest of the family might as well move out!
- You can't communicate without arguing.
- You're afraid you're losing her!

Moms, let me say two things to put your minds at ease:

#1: These are normal behaviors of teen girls!

#2: Your fears are valid. The world is out to destroy our girls, and it's important that we're aware of what they're up against.

On the Flip Side

These can be some of the most fun and memorable days of your lives if you look at the teen years with some perspective:

- Yes, there *will* be challenges—expect them and be ready for them.
- The teen years are *one* phase of her life. You *will* get through them. If you can be patient, she'll stop being so impulsive and self-centered, and you'll once again become smart!

In the meantime, there are some things you can do that will help keep your relationship with your daughter close during her teen years. Don't expect her to tell you this, but here's what she desperately wants from you, her mom.

She Wants You to Be There

Obviously, I don't mean be *with* her all the time, but when you're together, be there for her. I mean *really* there for her.

Ask yourself this question: When your daughter talks to you, do you *really* listen or are you distracted?

How many of you have had your daughter stomp out of the room in tears, complaining that you "never listen to me!"

I finally got this after hearing Kelly say to me many times, "Mom! You're not listening to me!" I really did hear every word she said, or at least I thought I did, but from her perspective I wasn't listening simply because I was doing other things as she was talking.

I had to make a point to stop what I was doing and look her in the eyes when she was talking to me.

Moms, this is so important. If your daughter even *thinks* you're not listening to her, she'll more than likely stomp out of the room and go find someone who *will* listen to her—whether it's her friends, the dog, the boy down the street who smiled at her on the bus, or possibly a stranger in a chat room.

She Wants You to Celebrate Who She Is!

Now, don't let this shock you, but she doesn't want to be a clone of you!

Is that news to any of you?

We have to remember, the teen years are full of questioning.

Your daughter is trying to figure out who she is and what her place is in the world.

When she rolls her eyes at you or has an emotional outburst, it's not that she hates you or is being rebellious—she's trying to figure out if what you've taught her is real.

She's been instructed in school to question everything. She may even question her faith and the values with which you've raised her. If you can realize this and not react to her in a moment of frustration, you'll save yourself a lot of stress.

Also, recognize that she may be different than you. **Your daughter may not be who you've envisioned she would be all these years.**

Her interests may be completely different from yours. That's okay! God created her to be unique—*one of a kind*.

Kelly and I are very different in many ways: She's a brown-eyed brunette—I have blue eyes and reddish hair. She has to be around people every chance she gets, while I often crave being alone. She's never met a stranger; I was shy and introverted at her age.

I think I know her style and taste, but I still end up returning nearly every gift I give her. It happened again just this Christmas—I shopped and shopped to find just what I thought she'd *love*, only to have her return it for something completely different.

We're very different, and we've had our share of conflict over the years. But here's the bottom line: We know we love each other and we're secure in that.

The truth is we all have preconceived ideas of who we want our daughters to become. You may have dreamed of her being a great gymnast or classical pianist only to discover she'd rather tinker with motors or ride a dirt bike!

Moms, one of the greatest gifts you can give your daughter is your support and encouragement to develop *her* interests even though they may be slightly disappointing to you.

You're her mom—the one person in the world she hopes she can count on when everyone else in her life lets her down.

Be patient with her during this time. If it's not a moral issue, let her try new things and experiment with styles and new interests. She'll eventually discover what she's good at and what fits her best.

I've worked with and counseled teen girls for a long time. Here's something I've discovered that will help keep your relationship strong:

Celebrate! *Make every milestone during these years a celebration of who she is and what she's becoming.*

If you get excited about what excites her, it will keep you connected with her and she'll *want* to share things with you.

For example, celebrate:

- The day she turns thirteen. She's been waiting for this day forever! Make a big deal of it! Throw her a party—give her a special gift.
- Getting her braces off—that's huge. Buy her a bag of gummy bears or a big bag of bubble gum!

- Her first boy-girl party or dance—take her shopping and let her pick out a new outfit.
- Making the volleyball team—cook her favorite dinner that night.

Make her feel special every chance you get!

We all feel like total failures at times when it comes to parenting our daughters, but if you make the effort to be open with her even before she becomes a teen, it'll be much easier for you to stay connected as she gets older.

Thanks for scooting next to the fireplace with me, moms. Now that we've had our heart-to-heart and have our favorite drinks in our tummies, let's talk about some other things that are important to your teen daughter.

Chapter 13

About God and Stuff

✉ I'm a Christian, so I don't understand why I feel so empty. It feels as if I'm losing God. Logically, I know He's right here with me, so what's going on?

✉ I've gone to church all my life. I believe in God and have a relationship with Him. But when I see all the people suffering from AIDS and wars and famine, I wonder where He is! Why would a loving God allow so much pain and suffering of innocent people?

✉ My friend died because she was hit by a drunk driver. Why did God allow that to happen?

✉ How do I know for sure that I'm a Christian? I think I'm saved, but I keep doing things I know are wrong and keep asking forgiveness. How do I know God really forgives me?

Most adults struggle with questions concerning God, so it's understandable that your daughter may be battling some spiritual doubts as well. Because this is such a wide topic, let's hit a few key areas with which most teen girls wrestle.

Feeling vs. Fact: Strive to help your daughter understand the significant difference between spiritual feelings and spiritual facts.

Fact: We won't always feel God, but if we're Christians, we can know beyond a doubt that He's with us.

Ammunition: "And surely I am with you always, to the very end of the age" (Matthew 28:20).

Discuss that at times she'll be keenly aware of God's presence. He'll feel so close, she can almost reach out and touch Him. Those times are great! Encourage her to cherish those valuable moments. But also explain there will be many other times when she won't feel anything. Does that mean she's lost her relationship with God?

To answer this, ask her about the sun. "Honey, there are days you definitely feel the heat of the sun, right? But there are other days you can't even see it. It may be hiding behind a cloud, or we may be in the midst of a snowstorm. Do you doubt the existence of the sun on the days you can't feel it?"

Give her time to answer, and then continue. "You don't always feel the sun—yet you know it's still there. It's the same way with God. Some days His presence will be especially close, and other days you may not feel Him at all. Don't base your relationship with Him on feeling; base it on fact. And the fact that He's always with you is stated in the Bible. Let's memorize Matthew 28:20 together."

How Can a Loving God Allow Pain?

Discuss the scene in the Garden of Eden when Eve ate the forbidden fruit (Genesis 3:1–6). God didn't plan sin. He could have kept Eve from eating the fruit, but because He loves us so much, He chooses to allow us the freedom of choice. If He forced us to love and obey Him, our devotion to Him wouldn't be real.

When Eve disobeyed God, sin entered the world. And the result of sin is a fallen creation. We have sickness, pain, death, war, famine, etc., because of sin

Your daughter may ask, "So if someone is really sick, is it because he has sin in his life?"

"No. Sickness is the result of a fallen creation, but good Christians still get sick. And Christians still age, battle disease, and die. We don't suffer from arthritis because there's unconfessed sin in our lives; we suffer the consequences of a fallen world."

"But why do innocent people get attacked?" your daughter may ask.

"No one is innocent. We were all born with sin. God doesn't cause our pain, but He allows it because we live in a fallen world. Someday we'll live in a perfect eternal world with Him, and there will be an absolute void of sickness, tragedy, evil, and death."

Blessed Assurance

Perhaps you remember the old hymn "Blessed Assurance." Read through the words to this song with your daughter.

Blessed Assurance

Blessed assurance, Jesus is mine!
Oh, what a foretaste of glory divine!

Heir of salvation, purchase of God,
Born of His Spirit, washed in His blood!
This is my story, this is my song.
Praising my Saviour all the day long.
This is my story, this is my song.
Praising my Saviour all the day long.

Perfect submission, perfect delight!
Visions of rapture now burst on my sight!
Angels descending bring from above
Echoes of mercy, whispers of love.
This is my story, this is my song.
Praising my Saviour all the day long.
This is my story, this is my song.
Praising my Saviour all the day long.

Perfect submission, all is at rest,
I in my Saviour am happy and blest;
Watching and waiting, looking above,
Filled with His goodness, lost in His love.
This is my story, this is my song.
Praising my Saviour all the day long.
This is my story, this is my song.
Praising my Saviour all the day long.*

Teach your daughter that she can *know* she's been forgiven if she has genuinely repented of her sins, placed her trust in Christ to save her, and established a relationship with Him.

Ammunition: "For the wages of sin is death, but the gift of God is eternal life in Christ Jesus our Lord" (Romans 6:23).

Discuss that God loves her so much that He sent Christ to pay the penalty of death for her sins, and Christ died willingly for her.

*Words by Fanny J. Crosby, 1820–1915; Music by Phoebe Palmer Knapp, 1839–1908.

Ammunition: "He himself bore our sins in his body on the tree, so that we might die to sins and live for righteousness; by his wounds you have been healed" (1 Peter 2:24).

God did this to prove His great love for us.

Ammunition: "For God so loved the world that he gave his one and only Son, that whoever believes in him shall not perish but have eternal life" (John 3:16).

It's all about trust. Here's what Christ says: "I tell you the truth, whoever hears my word and believes him who sent me has eternal life and will not be condemned; he has crossed over from death to life" (John 5:24).

Curiosity About Other Religions

✉ I have two stepsisters. I'm a Christian, but they're goth, and they worship Satan. I've heard not all goths worship the devil, but they do. I don't know how to deal with this.

✉ What's the deal with witchcraft? Is it really bad?

✉ How do I know that I should be Christian and not Muslim or Jewish or Buddhist? I don't doubt that Jesus is real, but how do I know He's really the One I should serve spiritually?

✉ I have some friends who are into Wicca. Is this okay? They say it's harmless. Is it?

✉ Why are people so tough on goths? I'm a Christian goth, and I use the darkness I've been through in a positive way to show others they can make it. My dark clothes, makeup, and hair just reflect the pain I've been through. This is my way of showing the world that I'm carrying my cross.

✉ Aren't all religions pretty much the same?

> ✉ I'm fifteen and a goth Christian. Obviously, this isn't a problem for me, but my parents are freaking out about it. They say I should get out of the goth scene because it makes people think I'm into witchcraft, drugs, and cutting, which I'm not and never will be.
>
> So why are my parents so hung up with all this? After all, isn't what you believe more important than what you look like? Hey, if people assume that I do bad stuff because of how I look, it's really not my fault. I just want to be different, and yeah, I do look like a tough, hardcore goth, but that doesn't give people a reason to judge me about my beliefs.

It's normal for your daughter to be curious about other religions. Assure her that Christianity can take all the doubts and questions she can toss its way or it wouldn't have lasted more than two thousand years.

Don't let her curiosity about other beliefs frighten you. Be willing to study the differences together, and help her realize that Christianity is genuine truth while the others are simply temporary philosophies.

A couple of great books to read together are the student editions of *The Case for Christ* and *The Case for Faith* by Lee Strobel. The author was an award-winning journalist who was so dismayed at his wife's conversion to Christianity, he decided to prove it was a hoax. During his research, however, he ended up becoming a Christian. Be sure you get the student editions of the books!

Help your daughter realize that Christianity is the only faith that serves a risen Savior!

Goth? Whew! That's kind of under this umbrella, and it's kind of on its own. What is goth? Different people will give a variety of definitions, but generally speaking . . . goth teens wear all black, including black lipstick and black nail polish, and often even dye their hair black. It's an outward expression of how they're feeling inside.

Many teens will say, "I'm a Christian, but the goth dress is simply my preference."

While we don't want to judge someone by outward appearances, it's only natural to judge a tree by its fruit. In other words, if your daughter claims she has a strong relationship with Christ and simply wants to dress gothic because that's her personal taste, watch for Christlike fruit. If you don't see it, you certainly have reason to question her motives.

For discussion: If we're in love with Christ, won't we want to reflect His joy, peace, and purpose not only in our actions but in how we dress as well?

In this section we've included more questions that most teen girls wrestle with in the spiritual category. Because of the importance of this chapter, we've decided to answer each question individually to give you extra resources as a mom when dealing with these hot spiritual issues. Also, until now, all the questions we've answered have been directed toward you, moms. But now we'd like to switch gears and answer these questions as if we're talking directly to your daughter. We encourage you to take our answers and make them your own so you can share them with your daughter.

✉ How can I tell right from wrong?

The Bible—God's Holy Word—is our source of guidance and truth. As Christians, we can use His Word to steer us in the right direction and keep us from making detours that would take us in the opposite direction.

Check this out: "The whole Bible was given to us by inspiration from God and is useful to teach us what is true and to make us realize what is wrong in our lives; it straightens us out and helps us do what is right. It is God's way of making us well prepared at every point, fully equipped to do good to everyone" (2 Timothy 3:16–17 TLB).

The Holy Spirit also guides us into truth. He's faithful to prick our conscience when we do something wrong and gives us discernment to know how to make wise choices.

✉ If God has truly forgiven me, why do I still feel so guilty?

Try to look at it as a *good* thing when you feel guilty for doing something wrong. This proves you have a tender conscience and that you're feeling the nudge of God's Holy Spirit within you. If you felt no guilt at all when you sin, you wouldn't be quick to seek forgiveness.

After you've repented of your sin, you can be assured that God *has* forgiven you, and you don't need to wallow in guilt. But let's chat for a second about repentance. In the Greek language, the word translated as *repent* means to turn the other way. In Bible days, if you saw someone going the wrong direction, you'd shout, "Jamie! Repent!" And Jamie would turn around and go the other way.

When we repent of our sins, it needs to be with the attitude of, "Oh, dear Father, I'm so sorry I've disobeyed you. I've broken your heart and sinned against you. Will you forgive me? I don't ever plan on going down that path again. In fact, I'm going to set up accountability and boundaries in my life to keep me from going that direction again."

That's genuine repentance. But sleeping with your boyfriend and casually saying, "Sorry about that, God. Will you forgive me?" and knowing you'll probably sleep with him again next week isn't genuine repentance.

If you've truly repented of your sins and have turned the other direction with God's help, He has forgiven you and you no longer need to feel guilty about your past. If you continue to live in guilt after you've been forgiven, that's false guilt. Memorize Romans 3:23–24 for proof of your forgiveness: "For all have sinned and fall short of the glory of God, and are justified freely by his grace through the redemption that came by Christ Jesus."

✉ I really want to share my faith with my friends who aren't Christians, but I'm scared they'll laugh at me or ask me a question I can't answer.

Being laughed at is a very real possibility. But you're not alone! The Bible is packed full of stories of those who were persecuted because of their faith. Most people, however, admire someone who stands tall because of her convictions.

Be honest with God. Tell Him you're afraid to share your faith. Ask Him to increase your confidence. Start small by simply inviting one of your friends to a youth group activity such as a pizza party or lock-in. It probably won't be long until your friend asks *you* about the difference in your life.

And remember: You're never alone. God has promised to be with you and strengthen you. Take a peek at what the apostle Paul told Timothy: "Preach the Word of God urgently at all times, whenever you get the chance, in season and out, when it is convenient and when it is not" (2 Timothy 4:2 TLB).

✉ Why doesn't God answer my prayers?

Guess what? You're in good company! The Old Testament prophet Habakkuk asked the same question. In fact, his little book is only three chapters long, and the first chapter is basically a list of questions: "Why do good people continue to suffer? Why do evil people seem to prosper? Why aren't you answering my prayers in regard to your people?"

The truth is, God *does* answer our prayers. He answers every single prayer we pray; He just doesn't always answer in the way we want Him to. And oftentimes He doesn't answer *when* we want Him to, but He always answers. Look at one of the answers He gave Habakkuk: "But these things I plan won't happen right away. Slowly, steadily, surely, the time approaches when the vision will be fulfilled. If it seems slow, do not despair, for these things will surely come to pass. Just be patient! They will not be overdue a single day!" (Habakkuk 2:3 TLB).

☒ Why did God make me so ugly?

Whoa! The Bible says that you were made in God's image (Genesis 1:27). There may be something about yourself you're not happy with (almost everyone feels this way, whether it's having too big of a nose, being too short, wishing for a different texture of hair, etc.), but that doesn't mean you're ugly.

Try to see yourself from God's point of view. You're not an accident! He created you—and He created you just the way you are to bring glory to His name. Ask Him to teach you how to love yourself like He does.

Check this out: "You turn things upside down, as if the potter were thought to be like the clay! Shall what is formed say to him who formed it, 'He did not make me'? Can the pot say of the potter, 'He knows nothing'?" (Isaiah 29:16).

In other words, why would you want to argue with your Creator when you know He is all-wise, all-loving, and perfect?

✉ I've been angry at God for a long time. I moved last summer, broke up with a boyfriend, and so far I haven't made any new friends. I know I need a relationship with God, but every time I pray I feel like I'm just saying words that I don't mean. After all, God's the One who brought the hurt here in the first place.

I believe there's a reason for everything, but I've been depressed for the past seven months. I talked to my youth minister and parents, but nothing has gotten better. What should I do to become less angry and not so depressed?

We feel for you. It's tough to leave your friends and move to a new place. But God didn't cause your pain. He's allowing you to experience loneliness right now, but there can be a good side to that! You've stated that you need a relationship with God. Use this time *right now* to grow closer to Him. You don't have anyone or anything to distract you from developing deep intimacy with Him, so take advantage of that. But keep praying that He'll bring some Christian friends across your path.

Maybe you're familiar with See You at the Pole. It's an annual event in which students across North America stand by their school's flagpole on the fourth Wednesday of September and pray for each other and their school. We encourage you to participate in this event, because it brings huge numbers of Christians out of the woodwork. It's likely you'll be able to establish friendships with some of the students there.

Also, strive to plug in to a Christian club on campus—Youth for Christ, Fellowship of Christian Athletes, a Bible study—and get involved in your youth group at church. These are great ways to make friends.

✉ Here's the deal: I feel like I'm a hypocrite. Yes, I'm a Christian, but God feels a million miles away. I have so many doubts about

God. Does He really hear me? Does He truly care about me and everything I'm facing?

Anything that concerns you concerns God. There's absolutely nothing too BIG and nothing too small to pray about. If God cares enough about you to know the number of hairs on your head (Matthew 10:30), He certainly cares about how you feel!

The Bible has some great advice about giving our problems to the Lord: "Cast all your anxiety on him because he cares for you" (1 Peter 5:7) and "Cast your cares on the Lord and he will sustain you; he will never let the righteous fall" (Psalm 55:22).

Yes, God cares, and even though He wants us to bring our problems to Him, there's also wisdom in sharing our problems with other Christians who can pray for us and give us wise guidance.

Consider talking with your parents, your Sunday school teacher, your youth leader, or another adult in your church.

Chapter 14

Relating to Your Teen Stepdaughter or Adopted Daughter

Perhaps you have a stepdaughter in your home, or maybe you've adopted a daughter. Sometimes this can bring another set of unique challenges. Let's look at both situations.

Your Teen Stepdaughter

Relating to your stepdaughter doesn't have to be as difficult as it may seem. Though it's a major transition for you to jump into the role of a stepparent, it's just as big (or perhaps even bigger) of a transition for your teen stepdaughter. Let's take a peek at some ways to make the transition smoother for both of you.

Tip #1: Accentuate the Positive

Your stepdaughter may be in your life now because her birth mother passed away or because of a divorce. Regardless of the reason, refuse to make negative or derogatory remarks about her mother. Consider purchasing a creative photo frame and presenting it to your stepdaughter so she can keep a current photo of her mother on display. Say as many positive things about her to your stepdaughter as possible. This will help your stepdaughter realize that you're a safe haven for her, and in time, she'll know she can talk freely about her mother with you. As this happens, the bond between you and your stepdaughter will become stronger.

Tip #2: Make Gradual Changes

If it's truly necessary to make changes in your stepdaughter's routine, don't make the changes sudden. Perhaps it's necessary to cut back on extras for financial reasons, and you're going to have to omit her ballet lessons. Sacrifice something from your own end first, and slowly bring up discussion of ballet (or the proposed change). Talk it through often. Be up front with her. Be honest about your reasons (financial, time constraints, etc.). This will help her understand the change and eventually come to accept it instead of blaming the break in her routine on you.

Tip #3: Create New Traditions

If there are some loved traditions your stepdaughter is used to, continue to make those events happen. For instance, if she's used to having ham at Christmas dinner, maintain that for her. If she's been allowed to open one present before the Christmas holidays, allow her to keep that privilege. Discuss with her the value of traditions and the comfort they bring, and that you don't want to rob her of her favorite customs.

But also tell her that you'd love to create some brand-new traditions with her. Maybe it's the two of you choosing a new Christmas ornament for the tree each year. Perhaps it's a special holiday drink the two of you make together (e.g., hot chocolate with ground peppermint or eggnog). Or maybe it's a snapshot of the two of you in the same spot each year. For example, you and your stepdaughter with a beach ball in your front yard. Next year at the same time, take another photo with the same prop. It will be fun to display them on the wall or the fridge year after year and view the changes you both go through during the next several years.

Tip #4: Don't Keep Your Love a Secret

Make it your goal to tell her "too much" how loved and special she is. Write her a note and stick it in her wallet, purse, or backpack. Put sticky messages on her bedroom mirror. Go to the trouble of mailing her a card. Tell her verbally every single day how much you love her, and let her know *why* you love her. Too many parents and stepparents assume their teens know they're loved, but I meet numerous teens who hear far too little the most valued words from a parent: "I love you!"

Tip #5: Pray. Pray! PRAY.

I'm assuming you're praying *for* your stepdaughter, but I also want to encourage you to pray *with* her. It may be uncomfortable at first, and she may be totally against the idea. But it's important to make it happen. Sit on the edge of her bed at night and thank God for her. Take advantage of driving her somewhere and thank God out loud for her. Let her hear you pray for her and with her often!

Your Adopted Teen Daughter

You may have struggled at one time to share the news of your daughter's adoption with her. When you finally got over that hurdle, you faced another one: She's feeling rejected because her birth mother placed her up for adoption. How you handle her feelings is critical in guiding her into a solid, confident self-image.

Tip #1: Her Feeling of Rejection Is Real

Don't try to downplay it. You may *feel* like saying, "How can you feel rejected when we've showered you with love for years?" Instead say, "You have experienced a tremendous loss in your life. It's okay to grieve that loss. Let's pray about that loss together. But let's also thank God for allowing your new family to fill the void you've experienced."

Tip #2: This Is Simply Part of Her Developmental Process

Your daughter may feel guilt for not being able to motivate her birth mother to stay (even though she was probably so young she can't remember her birth mother). Still, feelings of "Why wasn't I good enough to keep her around?" can haunt her.

You may *feel* like saying, "You can't possibly believe this is your fault! You were only a baby." Instead say, "I understand you wish you could change the past. And if you could, things might be different today. But you are a princess of the King of

Kings! He dreams big dreams for you. Let's ask Him to help you focus on the incredible future He has for you instead of replaying what might have been in the past."

Tip #3: Understand That Your Daughter Will Hurt

Even though she's never known her birth mom, she may say, "I miss her. I want her." You may *feel* like saying, "But your dad and I wanted you so very much!" Don't try to fix her pain. Allow her the freedom to hurt. Let her grieve the loss in her life. She doesn't even fully understand her own feelings at this point. Though you can't entirely understand her struggle, you can try to identify. Say something like, "I don't know exactly how you feel, but let me share with you about a time I felt lost, confused, and rejected."

Let her cry, and cry with her. Understand that when she acts angry, it may be because she doesn't know how to deal with the hurt. Pray together often, and consider getting Christian counseling for continued anger and rejection issues you may notice.

Chapter 15

"You're Eighteen . . . So What?"

Is your daughter playing the "age card"? As young as age twelve, many teen girls begin using the lines, "Just wait until I'm eighteen! Then I can do whatever I want, and I won't have to follow your silly rules."

Though turning eighteen is certainly a cause for celebration, it *shouldn't* give your daughter the misconception that she's now able to do whatever she wants. You're still the parent; she's still the kid.

Don't Make Waves

Too many parents are afraid of making waves, and in wanting to maintain a peaceful front, they compromise by not standing up and holding their ground as parents. I (Susie) recently spoke with the mom of a teen girl who was experimenting with drugs. She was desperate. "What do I do? Tell me!" she begged.

I encouraged her to remind her daughter how loved she was and that they'd work through this, but she'd have to have her total honesty about the entire situation. "I've already done that," she replied. "I thought she was being honest. I had no idea she was dabbling with marijuana again."

I suggested counseling. They'd already been there and done that. So the mom proceeded to inform me about youth culture. "You don't understand, Susie. This is the culture she lives in. She tells me that everyone has tried marijuana, and she doesn't see anything wrong with it."

I reminded her it was against the law. "That's what I told her," the mom said. "But she says that's stupid, and it's no worse than smoking a cigarette or drinking alcohol. She believes marijuana should be legalized."

God's Truth

"But it's *not* legal," I reminded her mom. "She may not think it's wrong to smoke pot, and she may not think it's wrong to steal a pack of chewing gum or lie or cheat on a test. But it doesn't matter what she thinks—these things are still wrong. She's living in a fantasy world if she won't accept the fact that she's breaking the law when she smokes pot."

"I just don't know what to do."

"There's more that's happening here than breaking the law," I said. "Her spiritual life is also in trouble."

"Well, a pastor told me I just needed to go with the flow," her mom said. "He told me most teens try some form of drugs, and most teens turn out okay."

What?!

I apologized for the "advice" she'd been given and secretly questioned this pastor's calling.

Be a Parent!

"I just don't want to make waves," the mom continued.

"She's still the kid, and you're still the mom," I reminded her. "Tell her as long as she lives in your house, she has to follow your rules."

"But she's eighteen! And she's constantly reminding me of that. I'm afraid she'll leave."

"That's where tough love comes in. Don't let her use the age card as a way to manipulate you and your husband into compromising your standards. Tell her you love her dearly, you'd die for her, but as long as she lives in your home, she'll abide by your rules. If she refuses to agree, she needs to leave."

Yes, I'm a little angry as I write this! I'm tired of teen girls controlling their parents. And I'm heartbroken by parents who are afraid to be the adult in their parent-teen relationship.

But there *is* hope!

Strategies for High Standards

Though your teen daughter may be fast approaching the age of eighteen, it doesn't mean your standards have to be compromised.

Alisha slammed her bedroom door and screamed through the wall, "You're so unfair! I can't wait till I turn eighteen."

Natalie threw her books on the kitchen table and turned to her dad. "Oh, yeah? I'm eighteen! Cut me some slack or I'll leave this rathole."

Though many teen girls use the age card to manipulate parental control, I (Susie) want to encourage you to stand tall and to continue implementing godly standards in your home. It doesn't matter whether your daughter is twelve, fifteen, or eighteen. Again, she's still the kid, and you're still the adult. And as long as she's living in your home, she's in your jurisdiction. You have a legal responsibility to make sure she obeys the law, and you have a spiritual responsibility to guide her with godly standards.

Starting at the Beginning

Perhaps you've established and maintained godly standards for years, or maybe you're just now beginning to implement those standards. The best place to start is at the beginning. *Make your standards known.* Let there be no doubt in your daughter's mind as to what you expect of her. Tell her your stand on alcohol, curfew, evening activities, and church attendance. Let her know it doesn't matter if she's sixteen or eighteen—the standards remain the same.

Make the consequences known. When your daughter fails to keep your standards, there should be consequences. I recently spoke with a couple of moms who knew their daughters were dabbling with marijuana. "Well, I really don't think she'll do it again," one mom said. There was no hint of consequences. When we break the standard, part of responsibility is learning to face the consequences. That may be a grounding, taking away car privileges, limiting phone calls or computer access, etc. But make your consequences known.

Remind her that you have her best interests at heart. "This hurts me more than it hurts you" is hard to believe when you're sixteen. But when your daughter is twenty-five, she'll understand. In the midst of the screaming, anger, and confusion, continue to let her know how much you love her and want God's absolute best for her.

Maintain Your Ground

And what if your daughter leaves? What if she runs to a friend's house who doesn't have as many rules? That's where tough love comes into play. STAND YOUR GROUND. Do *not* compromise your standards because your daughter threatens you. You're the parent; she's the kid. Remind her that she has a high calling on her life. Reinforce the fact that you have established godly standards in your home because of your accountability with Jesus Christ. Let her know it will kill you if she leaves, but if she refuses to abide by your rules, your house can no longer be her home.

Yes, this sounds mean. Tough love is always hard. But what's the alternative? Compromising your standards means allowing your daughter to manipulate you, and it threatens her relationship with God. Bottom line: You want your daughter in heaven for eternity. So make the effort right now to enforce godly standards in your home and pray they become a part of her lifestyle.

Chapter 16

You Said . . . She Heard . . .

You've probably experienced it.

In fact, all moms of teenage girls have experienced it.

You make a simple comment. Or you even compliment your daughter!

She completely misinterprets what you said, and an emotional tirade ensues. We'll call it "You said/She heard."

It started out as an innocent observation—your daughter changed her hair one day.

You said: "Oh, your hair looks different today." Meaning, you noticed and thought it looked cute.

She heard: "Your hair looks different and stupid." *I might as well not even try anything new; I'll just look dumb and people will make fun of me.*

You said: "Why don't you wear the pink shirt with that instead of the blue one?" Meaning, you think it would be adorable on her.

She heard: "What you're wearing isn't good enough." *I have no taste and don't know how to dress myself.*

You said: "You're not going to get your homework done if you watch that movie first." Meaning, you know she'll be too tired to finish her homework if she doesn't do it right away.

She heard: "You can't manage your time or be responsible to do your homework." *I'm too stupid to know that I have homework to do.*

You feel as though you might as well not say anything for fear that what you *do* say will be turned around and used against you. Nothing you say comes out right, and everything you say offends her.

Sigh.

What's a mother to do? You can't win for losing.

First, be encouraged that every other mother of a teenage girl is facing this too. You're not the only one exasperated by the lack of communication with your daughter.

Good news! There *are* some things you can do to make it easier to say what you mean and have your emotionally charged young daughter hear what you're really trying to say—without making each conversation a major catastrophe.

Think Before You Speak

Remember, your hormonal and quite possibly insecure young daughter is trying desperately to fit in with her peers. Pointing out anything about her that makes her feel inferior to someone else or conspicuous will immediately put her on the defensive.

Begin your comments about her clothes, hair, or appearance with something positive. Make her feel *good* about herself even if you have to bite your tongue about the one thing she's wearing that you think looks absolutely ridiculous. She's trying to figure out who she is and what her style is. Encourage her individuality even if it kills you.

Listen First, Talk Second

Don't offer your opinion unless she asks for it. Many teen girls stop talking to their moms because every time they do talk, they get a lecture when all they wanted was to talk. Sometimes your daughter just wants you to listen and not give her advice. Be okay with that. When she wants your advice about something, she'll feel free to ask if she knows you'll talk *with* her and not *at* her.

As you give your daughter freedom to talk to you without fear of being scolded or talked down to, she'll be more comfortable coming to you to share her most personal thoughts and feelings. Be approachable. That usually means listening more than you talk.

Ask, Don't Assume

Sometimes it's easy for parents to overreact when they don't really have all the facts. For example, your daughter comes home twenty minutes after her curfew, but before you give her a chance to explain, you assume she was simply disregarding your rules and doing something she shouldn't have been.

Your tirade about not being considerate and making you worry will quickly slam the door to any communication. Give her a chance to explain. Let her know you trust her and believe there must have been a good reason for her being late and that she should have called you. You won't feel quite so foolish when you find out she gave a ride home to a friend who had a flat tire. Make sure your daughter knows you trust her unless she gives you reason not to.

Try to Understand Her Feelings

By the time you become the parent of a teen girl, your own teen years are a distant memory. The responsibilities and demands of adult life have skewed your memory of what it was like to be her age. You now have bills to pay, a household to maintain, and more on your mind than whether or not your daughter will be invited to the slumber party that all the cool girls at school will be going to on Friday night. If she doesn't get invited it's not the end of the world—at least not *your* world.

Social survival is critical for a teen girl. Not being included can be as devastating to her as missing the clearance sale at your favorite department store is to you. Be sensitive to her feelings even though they may seem trivial to you.

Avoid Power Struggles

Sometimes moody girls say things just to rattle their parents. Before you overreact, take a deep breath and consider the source. The goal is open communication, not confrontation. Never deal with a potential argument if either of you are tired, hungry, or on your way out the door. Agree to discuss the situation at a later time when you can both think more clearly. Whenever possible, give your daughter the opportunity to determine the consequences of her behavior if inappropriate or disrespectful. If there are no consequences, the undesired behavior won't change.

Apologize if Necessary

Parents don't always do everything right. Nobody knows this better than our daughters! When you blow it, don't be afraid to seek forgiveness from her. This will teach your daughter that you're willing to own up to your mistakes and right a wrong. This is an essential life lesson to learn. Your daughter will respect you for it.

Most teen girls really do want to spend more time with their parents but often feel the time they have together ends in arguments and frustration. They also sometimes have difficulty expressing their feelings without being misunderstood, so they opt for not talking at all about things that are bothering them. What's the solution?

Sometimes it's easy: Spend more time doing fun things and just enjoying being together. Don't make every interaction with your daughter a major production. You don't have to talk about her grades or how messy her room is every time you spend time with her. Make it fun simply to be together!

Lecture as little as possible. In fact, make an effort not to lecture at all. Teens don't like being talked down to—talk to your daughter just like you'd talk to an adult friend. She will respond much better if you show her a little respect for having a brain and the capability to use it.

If you're like most parents, you find yourself reacting to your daughter just like your parents reacted to you, and you hated it! Think about this—really think about it and purposefully put into practice a new way of communicating with your daughter.

Sometimes it's not what you say, but how you say it. Avoid statements that put her on the defensive, such as:

"You never..."

"You always..."

"You're too young to understand."

"You don't need to know about that."

"I don't care what your friends are doing!"

"If you say that again, I'll..."

"Watch your mouth, young lady!"

"Where did you hear that?"

These types of reactions are sure door-slammers for any further communication with your daughter.

Instead, try a different approach that encourages conversation, like:

"That sounds important to you."

"What do you think about that?"

"Do you want to talk about it?"

"That's a good question."

"What did you think when . . . ?"

"How did that make you feel?"

"Did that scare you?"

"What would you do if you were . . . ?"

This type of interaction is inviting her to share her feelings and ideas in a safe environment and shows her that you value her opinions.

Bless, Don't Criticize

When you get down to it, what your daughter really wants from you is your blessing. To bless someone is to speak life into her in a positive and affirming way—to wish her well.

She wants you to be there for her, but not control her.

Love her for who she is; don't try to change her.

Accept your differences and encourage her uniqueness.

Don't cripple your daughter by making her feel as though she's not good enough just the way she is. She gets enough of that every day from her peers and the media.

Make her feel like she's *special* every chance you get. In the end, you'll be the one to reap the rewards of raising an emotionally healthy and confident young woman!

Last But Not Least

The most important thing you can do for yourself *and* your teen daughter is to *enjoy* these years together. Our girls grow up and are gone in the blink of an eye. Your attitude about how you'll experience these years with your daughter will make all the difference.

You know what else? Attitude is a *choice*. You can *choose* whether you're going to be frustrated and anxious during your daughter's teen years or whether you'll make them fun and memorable!

There *will* be bumps in the road—no doubt about it. But how you choose to handle those bumps will determine whether navigating the teen years with your daughter is a positive, fun time for both of you or a dreadful experience you can't wait to forget.

Your girl needs to know you love her and will always be there for her no matter what. *Tell her* you love her. *Show her* you love her. If you say it but your actions don't convey it, your words will be empty.

We were in the D.C. area recently for one of our all-day CLOSER: Moms & Daughters conferences. Leslie Koepke was closing her message. She talks about growing up in a household where she never heard the words "I love you" from her mom. We won't spoil the message for you in case you haven't been to a CLOSER conference yet, but God eventually helped Leslie gain victory *in spite of* the fact that Leslie never heard those three precious words from her mom. God empowered her to be victorious. At the end of her message, Leslie challenges moms and daughters to turn to one another and say, "I love you," and give each other a hug.

Probably no one else noticed—we were standing at the back of the auditorium—but we saw one mom-daughter pair standing with everyone else but refusing to look at each other, acknowledge one another, touch, or even speak to each other. The girl simply stood and looked around at all the other moms and daughters hugging. The mom just looked straight ahead.

Obviously, we don't know their story. But if their relationship is going to be healed, one of them will eventually need to take the initiative. *Moms, be the initiator!*

"Oh, that's easy for you to say," you may want to tell us. "I'm that mom. You have no idea how many times I've tried to reach out to my daughter only to be met with hate." Or, "I've tried hugging her, but she refuses to let me and just backs away. She's impossible to love."

Keep trying.

How many times has God given up on *you*? NONE!

When will He quit trying? NEVER!

So how many times should you give up on your girl? NONE!

When should you quit trying to reach her? NEVER!

"But even when she rejects me? And ignores me? And physically walks away?"

Yes. Even then. Especially then.

No, it's not easy. But love always goes the distance.

God does it for you.

You, then, imitate Him and do it for your daughter.

Appendix A

Self-Destructing
A Teen's Battle With Cutting

Imagine holding so much hurt on the inside that experiencing great physical pain on the outside would seem minor.

Chava was fifteen years old when she started hurting herself. "I had really low self-esteem," she says, "and I was always condemning myself." In an effort to take her mind off of the deep hurt she was harboring in her heart, Chava began cutting herself and burning her arms with a curling iron.

Why?

Chava's pain began right before she entered her teen years. "When I was eleven," she says, "my family moved to Israel. While on vacation at a beach, I was raped by a twenty-nine-year-old lifeguard."

She didn't tell anyone because since he offered her a ride, and she voluntarily got in the car with him, she assumed the rape was her fault. And she was embarrassed.

"I didn't know what to do with all that hurt," she continues. "It just wouldn't go away. It kept growing and gnawing at my insides."

Despite the nightmare she experienced at the beach, Chava enjoyed living in another country and learning about a different culture. "My dad is a rabbi," she says, "and my family loved being in Israel."

But when she turned fifteen, her dad decided to move the family back to the United States. "I didn't want to come back," Chava explains. "I became very bitter about having to move again—and having to move such a long distance. I was just getting used to the culture, the food, the climate, and the people."

Trying to Fit In

When Chava arrived back in the States, she felt like an outsider. "I spent a lot of time trying to figure out where I fit in," she remembers. "All my friends had changed. It was really hard to find common ground with anyone—even with my best friends. They all thought I was weird."

Chava discovered one of her friends had bulimia. "I had always carried a phobia about my weight," she says, "and the fact that my one friend was bulimic influenced me to obsess about my own weight."

Because Chava was still hiding the pain from being raped, it didn't take long for her to attempt to fill the void in her life by controlling her weight. She began throwing up three times a day and finally got to the point where eating anything made her physically sick.

Her parents noticed the changes in their daughter and tried to help, but because Chava was determined to continue hiding her pain, they were limited in what they could do. They *did*, however, get her into counseling.

The Hurt Won't Go Away

Not only was she dealing with her secret of being raped, her weight fluctuation, and the rejection from her friends, but Chava's grandpa shot himself and died a month after she had returned from Israel. "I saw him one day, and he died the next," she remembers.

"I didn't want to keep thinking about all the hurt inside me. I was desperate to get my mind off all the sadness and confusion I was feeling," she says. So one day at a friend's house, when Chava was fifteen, she took a sewing needle and scraped her hands and arms. "Later, I told my mom that my friend's cat had scratched me," she says.

"Part of me was thinking, *I can't believe I'm doing this*. But the other part of me was somehow able to numb the pain on the *inside* because now I was focusing on a different pain—a physical pain on the *outside*."

Is There Hope?

Chava was finally hospitalized for excessive cutting and because of a suicide attempt. She was diagnosed with major depression and was placed in a locked-down facility. "I felt very far from God," she remembers. "I kept thinking, *He won't love me. Why would He? I'm too unworthy. I'm worth nothing.*"

But Chava's parents and church family continued to love her and pray for her. When she was released from the hospital, she began attending a weekly women's Bible study with her mom. "It was four hours long," she says. "We'd bring our workbooks and read out loud and really dig into the Scripture."

Chava had loved dancing since she was a child, and one day the Bible study group was listening to some soft music during their prayer and worship time. "The song was 'El Shaddai,' " Chava remembers. "I've always loved that song. I felt God was touching me in a special way. During the next few minutes, I got up and danced the song for the women."

Afterward, the women surrounded Chava and prayed with her. "I gave God 100 percent," she says. "I gave Him everything! I can't go back to the hospital. I can't continue to self-destruct. I can't keep destroying the temple God has given me."

Is she still tempted? "I'll be honest," Chava says. "I still struggle with the temptation to cut myself. I'm still battling bulimia, but God is working with me. Some of my healing may take time, but He's not giving up on me. I've surrendered myself to His care, and with His help, I know I'll make it.

"I'm so much closer now to my parents," she says. "The biggest help they've given me is to make me realize they're not giving up on me. They hug me a lot. They smile with their eyes as well as their mouths, and they show me in a million ways that they love me.

"My parents bought me a journal and assured me that it was for all my private thoughts and that no one would ever read it unless I chose to share it. There's such a security in that. So I'm writing down my thoughts now," she says. "That really clears my head. I love to write poetry.

"Later, I go back and reread what I've written, and it helps me gain a clearer perspective of what I'm struggling with. I also try to listen to calming Christian music."

Appendix B

Journey Into Darkness

A Personal Struggle With an Eating Disorder

by Rebecca Rung

What began as trying to keep off a few pounds suddenly transformed into a life-threatening nightmare.

Ka-thud. Ka-thud.

Ka-thud. Ka-thud.

My heart beat slowly as tears poured down my face. I counted silently in my bed as I watched the second hand, nearly obscured in the darkness, tick around the face of the old-fashioned clock. *Ka-thud.* One. *Ka-thud.* Two. *Ka-thud.* Three. Forty beats to sixty ticks. I had to face the truth: I was slowly killing myself, and I didn't know how to stop.

"Jesus!" I pleaded. "Save me!"

Slowly, my thoughts turned from the ever-slowing beat of my heart to the blurred memories of the past nine months, a period of time that would change my life forever.

It Should Have Been an Adventure

"Bye, Mom. Bye, Dad," I said with teary eyes. I hugged each of them. "You know I love you."

It was September 2005, and I was leaving home for the first time to go to a Christian university eight hours north of my hometown. It was surreal for me to be saying good-bye. My family and I had always assumed that as the "mama's girl" of the clan, I'd stay close to home and go to the local university. But I felt God calling me north to obtain a Christian university education and, consequently, to temporarily say good-bye to my family. I knew it would be a tough transition, but I was about to find out exactly how tough.

The fourteen other girls in my dorm seemed nice enough at first. I tried to be outgoing—something which doesn't come naturally for me—but once orientation week was over and classes started, I found myself in my well-worn niche of unpopularity. I tried to fill the hole with high achievement, but I missed my family terribly and called home at least every other day and emailed as often as possible. I put on a happy face for everyone. I told my family and friends that I liked school and was doing well. But it was a lie.

Besides social struggles, I was also struggling against the so-called "freshman fifteen." I was terrified of gaining weight. I had grown up with a militantly nutrition-conscious mother, and I felt as though I had no excuse not to keep off the extra pounds.

Eating in the college cafeteria was a challenge. Everything I saw seemed to be loaded with fat calories. I longed for fresh veggies, but they were a rare commodity. My breaking point came in October when I saw that the number on my scale had risen one pound. I vowed that I'd not gain weight, no matter what it took.

And I held to that vow. I started looking up the calorie content of everything I ate and giving myself a mental calorie limit, which slowly waned to less and less. About twice a week, I'd lose control and eat everything I could get my hands on, but I always punished myself afterward, letting nothing but tea and diet soda touch my lips.

I got up at 6:20 each morning so I could run before class began at eight. I loved the feeling of control I got from running until I thought I was going to fall down, and then eating a few pieces of sliced melon for breakfast. I loved picking at a salad while watching my roommate chow down on pasta alfredo, patting myself on the back for my self-control. But what I loved most was seeing the number on the scale plummet. I lost nearly twenty pounds that year.

The Secret Is Out

Summer break approached, and Mom picked me up at college to drive me home. I was glad to be back with my family, but my normal routine had drastically changed from when I last lived at home. My new normal was now what I had created during my freshman year of college.

I literally thought about nothing but food, but I'd never allow myself to taste any of the things I fantasized about. The bingeing ceased almost completely as I allowed myself less and less food. My mom finally noticed something was up and got it out of me that I was not having my period. She hauled me in to see the doctor, who immediately diagnosed me with anorexia nervosa and had me set up regular appointments with a therapist and dietitian.

My life went downhill from there. Not only did I now have to deal with the anxiety I had whenever it came to eating, but I also had my parents ogling me, scrutinizing everything that went into my mouth. The combined pressure of trying to appease my eating disorder and my parents simultaneously was more than I could bear. I succumbed to depression and exhaustion, which allowed me to do almost nothing but lie on the couch for hours on end, sometimes crying, sometimes just staring blankly at the wall.

Recognizing the Truth

August came and I hit rock bottom. My turning point came as I was reading C. S. Lewis's *Mere Christianity*. He wrote, "The more we get what we now call 'ourselves' out of the way and let Him take us over, the more truly ourselves we become."

I shut the book, my mind racing with heavy thoughts. If that was true, I needed to give up the crutch of my eating disorder and let God fill the hole it left.

But was I ready?

What would I do without it?

Who would I be twenty pounds heavier?

Although the thoughts frightened me, I realized I had nothing left to lose. In the battle to keep my eating disorder, I had lost contact with nearly all my friends and all but destroyed my family relationships. Physically I was a ruin of my former self. I told my mom that I was ready to give in and went to bed still mulling over the words of C. S. Lewis.

Ka-thud.

Ka-thud.

Ka-thud.

Jesus, I can't do it anymore! I can't do it! I'm going to die! I'm too young! Help me!

I fell into a restless sleep, happy to forget my problems, even for just a little while.

What Next?

Having finally admitted that I needed help, I began to research alternatives to hospitalization, a choice which my doctor had suggested and I had rejected completely, leaving her office in a hysterical fit of screaming and crying.

I remembered seeing an advertisement in an issue of *Brio* a long time ago for a Christian eating disorder treatment center called Remuda Ranch. I looked it up and found what I was looking for: a former dude ranch converted into a treatment center for girls with anorexia and bulimia. All it took was a phone interview and I could be admitted.

Resigned to my fate, I gave my parents the Web address and told them that Remuda was the only treatment center I'd agree to attend. I woke up the next morning to the sound of my mother grilling the Remuda representative over the phone about the facilities, cost, program, etc.

The representative must have said something right because my parents were sold on the program. They set up a phone interview for me the following Wednesday, which consisted of forty-five minutes of solid questions about my past and present. When the questioning was done, I asked if I would get in. When the representative said that I probably would, I started crying. I was truly ready to give up my eating disorder and get on with my life.

I was admitted and would be leaving in a week's time. I spent the next few days packing and saying good-bye. I didn't even cry when I hugged my mom and stepped on the plane, which was a mark of how devastating my eating habits had been to our relationship. I was flying to Arizona and to a better life.

In the back of my mind, I was completely relieved that they were not going to let me exercise or allow me to restrict my eating. There was also a lot of fear in that prospect, but it was too late to turn back now.

Getting Well Takes Courage

I was met at the gate by a representative who took me directly to the ranch where I would be staying for the next forty five days. My first impressions weren't positive. The place looked like a house . . . an overcrowded house.

Girls sat on couches, on the floor, and anywhere else they could find space to color, play cards, sleep, or write letters. The girls were nice, though, and they all greeted me with genuine smiles and assured me that although the first couple of days were hard, it would get better.

I quickly discovered that they were right about the first few days being hard! I arrived in a wave of new admits, which had the staff bustling around like crazy. The first thing I did when I arrived was sit on the couch for half an hour waiting for someone to tell me what to do.

Finally the nurse came and had me put on a hospital gown. I was weighed and examined, and then it was lunchtime. I didn't usually eat lunch at home, or if I did, I'd simply have some vegetables or fat-free yogurt, but now I was starting again cold turkey.

I was led to a table with five other girls and a staff member, who all gave me reassuring smiles. I was presented with a turkey salad sandwich and an apple, which was terrifying to someone who was afraid of fat in all shapes and forms. I don't know how I managed to get it down, but I did. I felt afterward that I never wanted to eat again, but I did eat again at dinner that night. And, yes, that was just as hard for me as lunch.

That evening I was led to my room, where two staff members searched my luggage for any contraband items I could potentially use to practice my disorder. As I thumbtacked the photos of my parents onto my bulletin board, tears streamed down my face.

What am I doing here? I can't do this. I've never been able to make friends before, so why should I be able to make friends here? How am I going to survive forty-five days?

I slept fitfully that night and woke dreading breakfast—but I survived it. That day I also met my therapist, Shelley, and my dietitian, Amanda, who were very understanding. Amanda seemed to know where I was coming from and offered sympathy and encouragement, but when she mentioned weight gain, I trembled. I could barely manage a normal meal. How was I going to do that plus drink a supplement? Would I have to get a feeding tube through my nose like some of the other girls had?

The thoughts continued to race through my head as I headed toward the psychologist's office in a golf cart driven by one of the staff. There would be no walking around the grounds until I was medically cleared.

The psychologist was also wonderfully sympathetic, asking me why I had come, the history of my disorder, and other pertinent questions. Midway through the session I burst into tears, explaining between sobs that I missed home terribly and I didn't think I'd be able to drink a supplement and gain weight.

Friendships Are Born

When I returned to the house, I continued to sob until one of the girls came over and prayed for me. I was very encouraged by that. Most of the girls there had had their eating disorders much longer than I had, and they seemed to be getting through meals, snacks, and prescribed cans of supplement.

The girls were also right in saying that things were going to get better. I managed to not only eat three snacks per day, but I also worked up to drinking three cans of supplement per day. And I began to get to know the other girls, who, I was surprised to discover, knew exactly what I was going through and what I had done to get there: the lies, the days of hunger so extreme I felt I was going to faint, and the hopelessness of ever recovering.

Maureen, a thirty-seven-year-old woman who had arrived the day before I did, was particularly understanding. We quickly became friends, our common bond of suffering and our goal of recovery bringing us together.

Sonja, a bulimic girl from Eastern Europe, also became one of my close friends. She loved God very much and encouraged me not to abandon my faith. She was strong in the Lord, although her disorder was severe.

The other girls were the only thing that got me through treatment. I had to learn to open up to them in group sessions, but I never felt judged. I began to gain weight—something

I had to learn to accept each morning as I got out of bed to face the day.

But the biggest change was that I began to be happy—happier than I'd ever been in my entire life. For once, I had friends whom I was allowing to see the deepest parts of my soul, and they loved me anyway. God was definitely at Remuda Ranch!

The Work Begins

From the beginning, I knew there would be one week in treatment devoted to family therapy and healing the hurts that the eating disorder had caused within my family unit. It came too quickly.

I was told to prepare a list of hurts, apologies, and affirmations for each of my family members attending family week. My whole family was coming, so that made four. Each of my family members did the same.

The week began with speakers and seminars, but it centered on presenting our lists (called "Truth in Love") to our families. We were all extremely nervous, but I've never had a more freeing experience. We were able to cry together, forgive each other, and start over.

At the end of the week, I was sad to see my family go, but even sadder when I realized that I only had two weeks left until I would leave the ranch forever.

Settling In

After family week, time passed quickly. I was finally able to enjoy myself, eating meals normally, talking with my friends, and attending groups and activities. I didn't expect to have the time of my life in treatment, but that was exactly what was happening. As each day passed, I felt more and more confident in my recovery. In fact, I was beginning to feel invincible. However, God wasn't going to allow me to become complacent about recovery.

A new obstacle came up: making menus for home. As silly as it sounds to a normal eater, making menus was torture for me. For the first time in forty-five days, I was being forced to transition from simply thinking about eating food to concentrating on actually buying food! The task of purchasing food and then eating it all pushed me over the edge. I spent a sleepless night turning things over in my head before I burst into tears after breakfast the next day.

Maureen held me and encouraged me, as did Sonja. They suggested that I check into Remuda's transitional living program, Life. Up to this point, I hadn't planned on going to Life, to my therapist's displeasure, but this incident was more than enough to convince me of what I had to do.

It was terrifying to think of having to make friends all over again and, of course, eventually making new discharge menus, but I knew it was God's plan. And the good news was that money came in for Sonja to join me at Life.

Changes

Saying good-bye to Maureen, my therapist, my dietitian, Joker—my horse—and others was truly heartbreaking. My support group had a good-bye for me where they passed around a beautiful stone and offered encouragement. Whoever held the stone took the opportunity to share her thoughts. The stone finally ended on my lap. Of course, I cried.

And these tears were tears of fear that I'd never see these wonderful friends ever again. I didn't think I could live with that. I left the ranch for Life, which was two hours south, trying very hard to be optimistic about my future.

Despite the bitterness of that day, the best was yet to come, although not immediately. My arrival at Life was terrifying. I found myself (again) with few friends and no knowledge of what was going on or what I was supposed to be doing. There was a lot more freedom on the cul-de-sac of eight or so houses filled with girls just like me, trying to make a new life for themselves.

But I was still miserable about leaving my friends, therapist, and dietitian behind. I held on to the promise that Sonja would join me later that week, which ended up being my turning point. After her arrival, I began to have the time of my life. We went shopping together, played games, went to group sessions, went on walks, and hung out with our other friends. I even got to go to the zoo with one of the girls I met at Life.

My recovery was going so beautifully that two weeks into it, my therapist suggested I go to the independent living apartments, where I'd be accountable only to myself. Though I was sad and nervous to leave the girls in my house, I learned to love my apartment and the girls who lived with me. I'll admit that grocery shopping and menu planning was a bit daunting at first, but it soon became as natural as eating had become.

Transition

The day I was scheduled to leave, I cried for hours. The future seemed so unclear. I was going home to try and make friends who didn't have eating disorders and to learn to trust God through it all. I offered a hysterical good-bye to Sonja and the others, and I prayed as I boarded the plane.

Dear Lord, I know you have amazing plans for me. Please give me that hope for myself. Help me to learn to love who I am and present myself to you and others with no fear of rejection. Amen.

As the plane roared down the runway, I knew God was going with me. He is the Alpha and Omega, and He would see me through my recovery.

Becky is still seeing a therapist and dietitian and attends Oregon State University as a psychology major. Her goal is to return to Remuda Ranch someday to counsel girls who struggle with eating disorders.

For more information on Remuda Ranch: *www.remudaranch.com* or 1-800-445-1900.

www.goodtimesbooks.com

Have you enjoyed the book?
We hope, this book has helped you in
Rediscovering The New World